LAW, CRIME AND LAW ENFORCEMENT

HATE CRIME DATA COLLECTION

GUIDELINES, IDENTIFICATION ASSISTANCE AND SELECTED STATISTICS

LAW, CRIME AND LAW ENFORCEMENT

Additional books in this series can be found on Nova's website under the Series tab.

Additional e-books in this series can be found on Nova's website under the e-book tab.

LAW, CRIME AND LAW ENFORCEMENT

HATE CRIME DATA COLLECTION

GUIDELINES, IDENTIFICATION ASSISTANCE AND SELECTED STATISTICS

GLORIA THOMPSON
EDITOR

nova publishers
New York

Library of Congress Cataloging-in-Publication Data

ISBN: 978-1-63483-624-1

Published by Nova Science Publishers, Inc. † New York

CONTENTS

Preface		**vii**
Chapter 1	Hate Crime Data Collection Guidelines and Training Manual *Law Enforcement Support Section (LESS)* *Crime Statistics Management Unit (CSMU)*	**1**
Chapter 2	Hate Crime Victimization, 2004–2012 - Statistical Tables *Meagan Meuchel Wilson*	**69**
Index		**93**

PREFACE

This book is intended to assist law enforcement agencies in reporting incidents of hate crime to the FBI Uniform Crime Reporting (UCR) Program. It addresses policy, the types of bias crime to be reported, how to identify a hate crime and guidelines for reporting hate crime. Furthermore, this book presents counts and rates of hate crime victimization in 2012, using data from the National Crime Victimization Survey (NCVS). The tables show change in the number and rate of hate crime victimizations since 2011 and during the 10-year period since 2003. They examine the perceived motivation for the hate crime, demographic characteristics of victims and offenders, and the percentage of hate crime reported to police. In addition, the tables compare characteristics of hate crime and nonhate crime victimization, and the NCVS and FBI's Uniform Crime Reporting (UCR) hate crime statistics.

In: Hate Crime Data Collection
Editors: Gloria Thompson
ISBN: 978-1-63483-624-1

Chapter 1

HATE CRIME DATA COLLECTION GUIDELINES AND TRAINING MANUAL*

Law Enforcement Support Section (LESS) Crime Statistics Management Unit (CSMU)

PREFACE

On June 5, 2013, the CJIS Advisory Policy Board (APB) approved a motion to modify the Uniform Crime Reporting (UCR) Program's Hate Crime data collection procedures to begin including all self-identified religions in the United States as listed in the Pew Research Center's *Pew Forum on Religion and Public Life* (2008) and the U.S. Census Bureau's *Statistical Abstract* (2012). The APB also approved a motion to modify the UCR Hate Crime data collection procedures to include an anti-Arab bias motivation. The FBI Director authorized these motions on June 28, 2013. The FBI UCR Program, which collects and publishes information about crimes motivated by bias, has modified its data collection accordingly by defining the specific religions and the ethnicity/ancestry Arab, as well as providing corresponding examples. The UCR Program collaborated with members of the Arab, Hindu, Muslim, and Sikh communities to develop the corresponding training scenarios, as well as Appendix F.

* This is an edited, reformatted and augmented version of a document (Version 2.0), issued by the Federal Bureau of Investigation February 27, 2015.

This publication is intended to assist law enforcement agencies in establishing an updated hate crime training program so their personnel can collect and submit hate crime data to the FBI UCR Program. In addition to providing suggested model reporting procedures and training aids for capturing the new bias motivations, the manual is written to raise law enforcement officers' awareness of the hate crime problem. The FBI UCR Program is grateful to all who have assisted in preparing this publication.

1. Introduction

1.1. Purpose and Scope

This manual is intended to assist law enforcement agencies in reporting incidents of hate crime to the FBI Uniform Crime Reporting (UCR) Program. It addresses policy, the types of bias crime to be reported, how to identify a hate crime and guidelines for reporting hate crime.

Since 1991, thousands of city, college and university, county, state, tribal, and federal law enforcement agencies have voluntarily participated in the hate crime data collection. It is the law enforcement officers within these agencies who investigate offenses, determine those motivated by bias, and report them as known hate crimes that have made crucial contributions to the success of the hate crime data collection. Without their continued support and participation in identifying bias-motivated crimes, the FBI would be unable to annually publish *Hate Crime Statistics.* This partnership and, ultimately, this publication serve as the cornerstone in raising the nation's awareness about the occurrence of bias-motivated offenses.

1.2. The Nature of Hate Crime

In his work entitled, *Taking Rights Seriously,* Ronald Dworkin, Ph.D., stated that "justice as fairness rests on the assumption of a natural right of all men and women to equality of concern and respect, a right they possess not by virtue of birth or characteristics or merit or excellence, but simply as human beings." Dr. Dworkin's words reflect the Constitutional protections that are guaranteed to all Americans. And yet, there are those who are victimized, sometimes subtly and other times very overtly, for no reason other than the color of their skin, the religion they profess, the heritage of their parents, the disability they possess, their sexual orientation, their gender, or their gender identity. Not only is the individual who is personally touched by these offenses victimized, but the entire class of individuals residing in the community is affected.

1.3. Background

1.3.1. Legislative Mandate to Report Hate Crime

In response to a growing concern about hate crimes, on April 23, 1990, Congress passed the Hate Crime Statistics Act. This law required the Attorney General to collect data "about crimes that manifest evidence of prejudice based on race, religion, sexual orientation, or ethnicity." The Attorney General delegated the responsibilities of developing the procedures for implementing, collecting, and managing hate crime data to the Director of the FBI, who in turn assigned the tasks to the FBI UCR Program.

Under the direction of the Attorney General and with the cooperation and assistance of many local and state law enforcement agencies, the FBI UCR Program created a hate crime data collection to comply with the congressional mandate. The FBI UCR Program's first publication on the subject was *Hate Crime Statistics, 1990: A Resource Book,* which was a compilation of hate crime data reported by 11 states that had collected them under state authority in 1990 and were willing to offer their data as a prototype. The program continued to work with agencies familiar with investigating hate crimes and collecting related information so it could develop and implement a more uniform method of data collection on a nationwide scale. *Hate Crime Statistics, 1992,* presented the first data reported by law enforcement agencies across the country that participated in the UCR hate crime data collection.

1.3.2. Developing a Collection Approach

The primary emphasis in developing an approach for collecting national hate crime statistics was to avoid placing major new reporting burdens on law enforcement agencies contributing data to the FBI UCR Program. To accomplish this goal the following decisions were made:

1.3.2.1. The Hate Crime Data Collection Is an Adjunct to the UCR Collection

Hate crimes are not separate, distinct crimes, but rather traditional offenses motivated by the offender's bias. For example, an offender may commit arson because of his or her racial bias. It is, therefore, unnecessary to create a whole new crime category. To the contrary, hate crime data can be collected by merely capturing additional information about offenses already being reported to the FBI UCR Program.

1.3.2.2. The Types of Bias Motivation to Be Reported Are Limited

There are many kinds of bias. Some of the more common kinds are those against race, sexual orientation, or religion. There are also biases against rich people, poor people, the elderly, people who dress differently, smokers, drinkers, people who are overweight, etc. The types of bias to be reported to the FBI UCR Program are limited to those mandated by the Hate Crime Statistics Act and its subsequent amendments.

1.3.2.3. Two-Tier Decision-Making Process

Once the development of this collection was complete, the FBI UCR Program surveyed state UCR Program managers on hate crime collection procedures used at various law enforcement agencies which collected hate crime data employing a two-tier decision-making process. The first level is the law enforcement officer who initially responds to the alleged hate crime incident, i.e., the "responding officer" (or "first-level judgment officer"). It is the responsibility of the responding officer to determine whether there is any indication that the offender was motivated by bias. If a bias indicator is identified, the officer designates the incident as a "suspected bias-motivated crime" and forwards the case file to a "second-level judgment officer/unit." (In smaller agencies this is usually a person specially trained in hate crime matters, while in larger agencies it may be a special unit.)

It is the task of the second-level judgment officer/unit to review the facts of the incident and make the final determination of whether a hate crime has actually occurred. If so, the incident is to be reported to the FBI UCR Program as a bias-motivated crime.

1.3.2.4. Amendments Expand the Hate Crime Data Collection

Lawmakers amended the Hate Crime Statistics Act to include bias against persons with disabilities by passing the Violent Crime and Law Enforcement Act of 1994 in September of that year. The FBI started gathering data for the additional bias type on January 1, 1997. Next, the Church Arson Prevention Act, which was signed into law in July 1996, removed the sunset clause from the original statute and mandated that the hate crime data collection become a permanent part of the FBI UCR Program. Finally, in October 2009, the Matthew Shepard and James Byrd, Jr. Hate Crimes Prevention Act amended the Hate Crime Statistics Act under Division E of P.L. 111-84, the *National Defense Authorization Act for Fiscal Year 2010*. As a result, the FBI UCR Program now captures statistics on hate crimes based on gender and gender identity prejudices, as well as hate crimes committed by/directed against juveniles. (Appendix A provides the referenced legislation as amended.)

1.4. Conclusion

The enactment of the Hate Crime Statistics Act of 1990 and its subsequent amendments requiring the collection and publication of nationwide hate crime statistics underscores the emphasis placed on hate crime. National statistics have resulted in greater awareness and understanding of the true dimensions of the problem nationwide. Those charged with the enforcement of the law will be better able to quantify their resource needs and direct available resources to the areas where they will have the most effectiveness. Likewise, community service organizations and groups will be better able to respond to the needs of the victims.

2. Criteria of a Hate Crime

2.1. Bias Motivation

The FBI Uniform Crime Reporting (UCR) Program collects hate crime data regarding criminal offenses motivated, in whole or in part, by the offender's bias against a race, religion, disability, sexual orientation, ethnicity, gender, or gender identity. Due to the difficulty of ascertaining the offender's subjective motivation, bias is to be reported *only if* investigation reveals sufficient objective facts to lead a reasonable and prudent person to conclude that the offender's actions were motivated, in whole or in part, by bias. The specific types of bias to be reported, along with their UCR bias codes, are listed below. (More information about some types of biases is provided in Section 6.3, Learning Module Two.)

Table 1. Bias Motivation by Category and Type

Bias Category	Bias Motivation and code
Race/Ethnicity/Ancestry	Anti-American Indian or Alaska Native (13)
	Anti-Arab (31)
	Anti-Asian (14)
	Anti-Black or African American (12)
	Anti-Hispanic or Latino (32)
	Anti-Multiple Races, Group[1] (15)
	Anti-Native Hawaiian or Other Pacific Islander (16)
	Anti-Other Race/Ethnicity/Ancestry (33)
	Anti-White (11)
Religion	Anti-Buddhist (83)
	Anti-Catholic (22)
	Anti-Eastern Orthodox (81)
	Anti-Hindu (84)
	Anti-Islamic (Muslim) (24)
	Anti-Jehovah's Witness (29)
	Anti-Jewish (21)
	Anti-Mormon (28)
	Anti-Multiple Religions, Group (26) [1]
	Anti-Other Christian (82)
	Anti-Other Religion (25)
	Anti-Protestant (23)
	Anti-Sikh (85)
	Anti-Atheism/Agnosticism (27)
Sexual Orientation	Anti-Bisexual (45)
	Anti-Gay (Male) (41)
	Anti-Heterosexual (44)
	Anti-Lesbian (42)
	Anti-Lesbian, Gay, Bisexual, or Transgender (Mixed Group)[2]
Disability	Anti-Mental Disability (52)
	Anti-Physical Disability (51)
Gender	Anti-Female (62)
	Anti-Male (61)
Gender Identity	Anti-Gender Nonconforming (72)
	Anti-Transgender (71)

[1]Anti-Multiple Races, Group is reported if more than one victim in the incident is a different race. This also applies to the Anti-Multiple Religions, Group category.

[2]Lesbian, Gay, Bisexual or Transgender is referred to as LGBT.

2.2. Objective Evidence That the Crime Was Motivated by Bias

An important distinction must be made when reporting a hate crime. The mere fact the offender is biased against the victim's actual or perceived race, religion, disability, sexual orientation, ethnicity, gender, and/or gender identity does not mean that a hate crime was involved. Rather, the offender's criminal act must have been motivated, in whole or in part, by his or her bias.

Motivation is subjective, therefore, it is difficult to know with certainty whether a crime was the result of the offender's bias. For that reason, before an incident can be reported as a hate crime, sufficient objective facts must be present to lead a reasonable and prudent person to conclude that the offender's actions were motivated, in whole or in part, by bias. While no single fact may be conclusive, facts such as the following, particularly when combined, are supportive of a finding of bias:

1) The offender and the victim were of a different race, religion, disability, sexual orientation, ethnicity, gender, and/or gender identity. For example, the victim was African American and the offender was white.
2) Bias-related oral comments, written statements, or gestures were made by the offender indicating his or her bias. For example, the offender shouted a racial epithet at the victim.
3) Bias-related drawings, markings, symbols, or graffiti were left at the crime scene. For example, a swastika was painted on the door of a synagogue, mosque, or LGBT center.
4) Certain objects, items, or things which indicate bias were used. For example, the offenders wore white sheets with hoods covering their faces or a burning cross was left in front of the victim's residence.
5) The victim is a member of a specific group that is overwhelmingly outnumbered by other residents in the neighborhood where the victim lives and the incident took place.
6) The victim was visiting a neighborhood where previous hate crimes had been committed because of race, religion, disability, sexual orientation, ethnicity, gender, or gender identity and where tensions remained high against the victim's group.
7) Several incidents occurred in the same locality, at or about the same time, and the victims were all of the same race, religion, disability, sexual orientation, ethnicity, gender, or gender identity.

8) A substantial portion of the community where the crime occurred perceived that the incident was motivated by bias.
9) The victim was engaged in activities related to his or her race, religion, disability, sexual orientation, ethnicity, gender, or gender identity. For example, the victim was a member of the National Association for the Advancement of Colored People (NAACP) or participated in an LGBT pride celebration.
10) The incident coincided with a holiday or a date of significance relating to a particular race, religion, disability, sexual orientation, ethnicity, gender, or gender identity, e.g., Martin Luther King Day, Rosh Hashanah, or the Transgender Day of Remembrance.
11) The offender was previously involved in a similar hate crime or is a hate group member.
12) There were indications that a hate group was involved. For example, a hate group claimed responsibility for the crime or was active in the neighborhood.
13) A historically-established animosity existed between the victim's and the offender's groups.
14) The victim, although not a member of the targeted racial, religious, disability, sexual orientation, ethnicity, gender, or gender identity group, was a member of an advocacy group supporting the victim group.

2.3. Cautions

Need for Case-by-Case Assessment of the Facts—The aforementioned factors are not all-inclusive of the types of objective facts which evidence bias motivation. Therefore, reporting agencies must examine each case for facts which clearly provide evidence that the offender's bias motivated him/her to commit the crime.

Misleading Facts—Agencies must be alert to misleading facts. For example, the offender used an epithet to refer to the victim's race, but the offender and victim were of the same race.

Feigned Facts—Agencies must be alert to evidence left by the offenders which is meant to give the false impression that the incident was motivated by bias. For example, students of a religious school vandalize their own school, leaving anti-religious statements and symbols on its walls in the hope that they will be excused from attending class.

Offender's Mistaken Perception—Even if the offender was mistaken about the victim's race, religion, disability, sexual orientation, ethnicity, gender, or gender identity, the offense is still a hate crime as long as the offender was motivated, in whole or in part, by bias against that group. For example, a middle-aged, heterosexual man walking by a bar frequented by gay men was attacked by six teenagers who mistakenly believed the victim had left the bar and was gay.

Although the offenders were wrong on both counts, the offense is a hate crime because it was motivated by the offenders' anti-gay bias.

Changes in Findings of Bias—If, after an initial incident report was submitted, a contrary finding regarding bias occurs, during the course of the investigation, the FBI UCR Program file must be updated with the new finding. For example, if an initial finding of no bias was later changed to racial bias or a finding of racial bias was later changed to religious bias, the change should be reported to the FBI UCR Program. However, an agency should not update its report based on the findings of a court, coroner, or jury or the decision of a prosecutor.

3. Definitions for Hate Crime Data Collection

To ensure uniformity in reporting nationwide, the FBI Uniform Crime Reporting (UCR) Program has adopted the following definitions for use in hate crime reporting. When possible, source documents from which the definitions were derived are provided in parenthesis. In addition, parts of speech are given for newer terminology.

3.1. General Program Terms

Bias–A preformed negative opinion or attitude toward a group of persons based on their race, religion, disability, sexual orientation, ethnicity, gender, or gender identity.

Bias Crime–A committed criminal offense that is motivated, in whole or in part, by the offender's bias(es) against a race, religion, disability, sexual orientation, ethnicity, gender, or gender identity; also known as Hate Crime.

Note: Even if the offender was mistaken in his or her perception that the victim was a member of the group he or she was acting against, the offense is still a bias crime because the offender was motivated by bias against the group.

Hate Crime–Bias Crime.

Hate Group–An organization whose primary purpose is to promote animosity, hostility, and malice against persons of or with a race, religion, disability, sexual orientation, ethnicity, gender, or gender identity which differs from that of the members or the organization, e.g., the Ku Klux Klan, American Nazi Party.

National Incident–Based Reporting System (NIBRS)–A reporting system implemented in the late 1980s to replace the traditional Summary Reporting System (SRS) in reporting Uniform Crime Reporting (UCR) data. NIBRS provides for expanded collection and reporting of offenses and arrests and their circumstances.

Summary Reporting System–The traditional tally system which has been used since 1930 to collect UCR data.

3.2. Disability Bias and Associated Terms

Disability Bias–A preformed negative opinion or attitude toward a group of persons based on their physical or mental impairments, whether such disability is temporary or permanent, congenital or acquired by heredity, accident, injury, advanced age, or illness.

Mental Disability–Any mental impairment or psychological disorder such as: organic brain syndrome, emotional or mental illness, and specific learning disabilities. (Americans with Disabilities Act)

Physical Disability–Any physical impairment; any physiological disorder or condition, cosmetic disfigurement, or anatomical loss affecting one or more of the following body systems: neurological, musculoskeletal, special sense organs, respiratory (including speech organs), cardiovascular, reproductive, digestive, genitourinary, hemic and lymphatic, skin, and endocrine. (Americans with Disabilities Act)

3.3. Gender Bias and Associated Terms

Gender Bias—(noun) A preformed negative opinion or attitude toward a person or group of persons based on their actual or perceived gender, i.e., male or female.

Gender—(noun) This term is used synonymously with sex to denote whether a newborn is male or female at birth, e.g., "it's a boy" or "it's a girl."
Male – An individual that produces small usually motile gametes (as spermatozoa or spermatozoids) which fertilize the egg of a female. (Merriam-Webster Dictionary)
Female – An individual of the sex that bears young or produces eggs. (Merriam-Webster Dictionary)

3.4. Gender Identity Bias and Associated Terms

Gender Identity Bias–A preformed negative opinion or attitude toward a person or group of persons based on their actual or perceived gender identity, e.g., bias against transgender or gender nonconforming individuals.

Gender Identity–(noun) A person's internal sense of being male, female, or a combination of both; that internal sense of a person's gender may be different from the person's gender as determined at birth.

Note: A transgender person may express their gender identity through gender characteristics, such as clothing, hair, voice, mannerisms, or behaviors that do not conform to the gender-based expectations of society.

Gender Nonconforming–(adjective) Describes a person who does not conform to the gender-based expectations of society, e.g., a woman dressed in traditionally male clothing or a man wearing makeup.

Note: A gender nonconforming person may or may not be a lesbian, gay, bisexual, or transgender person but may be perceived as such. Additional information is provided in Appendix E.

Transgender–(adjective) Of or relating to a person who identifies as a different gender from their gender as determined at birth.

Note 1: The person may also identify himself or herself as "transsexual." Additional information is provided in Appendix E.

Note 2: A transgender person may outwardly express his or her gender identity all of the time, part of the time, or none of the time; a transgender person may decide to change his or her body to medically conform to his or her gender identity.

3.5. Race/Ethnicity/Ancestry Bias and Associated Terms

Note: When the FBI's Hate Crime Statistics Program was initially implemented, racial bias was reported as a separate category and ethnicity bias was reported as ethnicity/national origin bias. It was then modified by the Office of Management and Budget's (OMB's) *1997 Revision to the Standards for the Classification of Federal Data on Race and Ethnicity.* With the revised race and ethnicity categories and the addition of an ancestry (a subcategory of ethnicity), the OMB advised the program to publish the data in the combined category of Race/Ethnicity/Ancestry Bias.

Racial Bias–A preformed negative opinion or attitude toward a group of persons who possess common physical characteristics, e.g., color of skin, eyes, and/or hair, facial features, etc., genetically transmitted by descent and heredity which distinguish them as a distinct division of humankind, e.g., Asians, Blacks or African Americans, Whites.

Ethnicity Bias–A preformed negative opinion or attitude toward a group of people whose members identify with each other, through a common heritage, often consisting of a common language, common culture (often including a shared religion) and/or ideology that stresses common ancestry. The concept of ethnicity differs from the closely related term *race* in that "race" refers to grouping based mostly upon biological criteria, while "ethnicity" also encompasses additional cultural factors.

Ancestry Bias–A preformed negative opinion or attitude toward a group of people based on their common lineage or descent.

Race/Ethnicity/Ancestry Bias Types

American Indian or Alaska Native–A person having origins in any of the original peoples of North and South America (including Central America) and who maintains tribal affiliation or community attachment. This category includes persons from the following tribal affiliations: Navajo, Blackfeet, Inupiat, Yup'ik, or Central American Indian groups or South American Indian groups. (Census)

Arab–A person having origins, and/or ancestry, in any of the Arabic speaking peoples of Lebanon, Syria, Palestine, Jordan, Iraq, Saudi Arabia, Yemen, Oman, United Arab Emirates, Qatar, Bahrain, Kuwait, Egypt, Libya, Tunisia, Comoros, Algeria, Morocco, Sudan, Djibouti, Mauritania, and Somalia.

Asian–A person having origins in any of the original peoples of the Far East, Southeast Asia, or the Indian subcontinent including, for example, Cambodia, China, India, Japan, Korea, Malaysia, Pakistan, the Philippine Islands, Thailand, and Vietnam. This category includes persons from the following nationalities: Asian Indian, Bangledeshi, Bhutanese, Bermese, Cambodian, Chinese, Filipino, Hmong, Indonesian, Japanese, Korean, Laotian, Malaysian, Nepalese, Pakistani, Sri Lankan, Taiwanese, Thai, Vietnamese, Other Asian, specified; Other Asian, not specified. (Census)

Black or African American–A person having origins in any of the Black racial groups of Africa. This category includes persons from the following nationalities or groups: African American, Kenyan, Nigerian, or Haitian. (Census)

Hispanic or Latino–A person of Cuban, Mexican, Puerto Rican, South or Central American, or other Spanish culture or origin, regardless of race. Includes people from Hispanic or Latino groups such as: Dominican Republic; Central American (excludes Mexican)–Costa Rican, Guatemalan, Honduran, Nicaraguan, Panamanian, Salvadoran, Other Central American; South America–Argentinian, Bolivian, Chilean, Columbian, Ecuadorian, Paraguayan, Peruvian, Uruguayan, Venezuelan, Other South American; Spaniard–All other Hispanic or Latino.

Multiple Races, Group–A group of persons having origins from multiple racial categories.

Native Hawaiian or Other Pacific Islander–A person having origins in any of the original peoples of Hawaii, Guam, Samoa, or other Pacific Islands. This category includes persons from the following nationalities: Fijian, Guamanian or Chamorro, Marshallese, Native Hawaiian,

Other Micronesian, Other Pacific Islander, not specified; Other Polynesian, Samoan, Tongan. (Census)

Other Race/Ethnicity/Ancestry–A person of a different race/ethnicity/ancestry than is otherwise included in this combined category.

White–A person having origins in any of the original peoples of Europe, the Middle East, or North Africa. This category includes persons from the following nationalities: Irish, German, Italian, Lebanese, Arab, Moroccan, or Caucasian. (Census)

3.6. Religious Bias and Associated Terms

Religious Bias–A preformed negative opinion or attitude toward a group of persons who share the same religious beliefs regarding the origin and purpose of the universe and the existence or nonexistence of a supreme being, e.g., Catholics, Jews, Protestants, atheists.

> **Note 1:** The following list of religions represents most of the major religions in the United States. A general explanation is provided for each religion. Neither this list of religions nor the definitions provided are all-inclusive.
>
> **Note 2:** In many instances, a law enforcement officer will become aware of a victim's religious affiliation by information provided by the victim (i.e., self-reporting) or by people who have a personal relationship with the victim.

Agnostic–A person who believes that the existence or nature of an ultimate reality, such as a deity, is unknown, and probably unknowable. (Merriam-Webster Collegiate Dictionary [Eleventh Edition, 2003]; the Encyclopedia Britannica Micropedia Ready Reference [15th Edition, 2010])

Atheist–A person who does not believe in the existence of a deity. (Merriam-Webster Collegiate Dictionary [Eleventh Edition, 2003]; the Encyclopedia Britannica Micropedia Ready Reference [15th Edition, 2010])

Buddhist–A person who follows the religion of eastern or central Asia that grew out of the teaching of Siddhartha Gautama, the Buddha, or Enlightened One. People of this faith believe that suffering is inherent in life and that one can be liberated from it by mental and moral self-purification by following the Four Noble Truths and the Eightfold Path in order to reach *nirvana*. (Merriam-Webster Collegiate Dictionary [Eleventh Edition, 2003]; the Encyclopedia Britannica Micropedia Ready Reference [15th Edition, 2010])

Catholic–A person who follows the monotheistic religion of Catholic Christianity, especially that of the Roman Catholic Church. Followers of this faith believe the teachings of the Bible, and place emphasis on church traditions, including the historical continuity of the church, the Pope as the head of the church, and the requirement of celibacy of those in the priesthood. (Merriam-Webster Collegiate Dictionary [Eleventh Edition, 2003]; the Encyclopedia Britannica Micropedia Ready Reference [15th Edition, 2010])

Eastern Orthodox (Russian, Greek, Other)–A person who follows the monotheistic religion of the Eastern Christian Church. This faith follows the teachings of the Bible and church traditions, accords primacy of honor to the Patriarch of Constantinople as head of the church, and adheres to the decisions of the First Seven Ecumenical Councils and the Byzantine Rite. (Merriam-Webster Collegiate Dictionary [Eleventh Edition, 2003]; the Encyclopedia Britannica Micropedia Ready Reference [15th Edition, 2010])

Hindu–A person who observes the traditions and practices of the dominant religion of India, which include acceptance of the sanctity of the *Vedas* (sacred texts); the understanding of one Divine Reality manifested in multiple forms; acceptance of the laws of karma (principle of cause and effect), *dharma* (righteous modes of conduct), belief in reincarnation, and the ultimate spiritual goal of enlightenment (moksha). (The Encyclopedia Britannica Micropedia Ready Reference [15th Edition, 2010])

Islamic (Muslim)–A person who follows the monotheistic religion of Muslims, which includes belief in Allah as the sole deity and in Muhamad as his prophet. Practitioners of the Islamic faith follow the teachings of the Koran and practice the Five Pillars of Islam: praying, fasting during Ramadan, almsgiving, pilgrimage, and declaration of faith. (Merriam-Webster Collegiate Dictionary [Eleventh Edition, 2003]; the Encyclopedia Britannica Micropedia Ready Reference [15th Edition, 2010])

Jehovah's Witness–A person who follows the religion founded by Charles Taze Russell. Members witness by distributing literature and by personal evangelism of beliefs in the theocratic rule of God, the sinfulness of organized religions and governments, and an imminent millennium. The activities of Jehovah's Witnesses are governed by the Watchtower Society which makes all major decisions, interprets the Bible, and counsels Witnesses using Watchtower materials. Members of the faith are often seen giving generously of their time in proclaiming their faith and teaching in private homes. (Merriam-Webster Collegiate Dictionary [Eleventh Edition, 2003]; the Encyclopedia Britannica Micropedia Ready Reference [15th Edition, 2010])

Jewish (Judaism)–A person who identifies himself or herself as a member of the religious and/or ethnic group that descended from the ancient Hebrews and is characterized by belief in one transcendent God who revealed Himself to Abraham, Moses, and the Hebrew prophets. Jewish religious practice is based on the Hebrew Scriptures (the "Torah") and rabbinic laws and customs. (Merriam-Webster Collegiate Dictionary [Eleventh Edition, 2003]; the Encyclopedia Britannica Micropedia Ready Reference [15th Edition, 2010])

Mormon (Latter-day Saint)–A person who follows the Church of Jesus Christ of Latter-day Saints tracing its modern origin to Joseph Smith and accepting the Book of Mormon as scripture. Latter-day Saints consider the following writings to be scripture: 1) The Holy Bible; 2) The Book of Mormon, Another Testament of Jesus Christ; 3) The Doctrine and Covenants; and 4) The Pearl of Great Price. Mormons are often associated with members of the faith who serve as full-time volunteer missionaries in the U.S. and abroad. (Merriam-Webster Collegiate Dictionary [Eleventh Edition, 2003]; the Encyclopedia Britannica Micropedia Ready Reference [15th Edition, 2010])

Multiple Religions, Group–A group of persons demonstrating a commitment or devotion to religious faith or observance based upon multiple faiths.

Other Christian–A person who follows other denominations or nondenominational religions based on the life and teachings of Jesus Christ but not described above. Examples of these religions include Metaphysical-Christ Church Unity, Spiritualist, Unity/Unitarianist, Unity Church, Universalist, and Other Metaphysical. (Pew Research Center)

Other Religions–A person who follows other non-Christian religions not described above. Examples of these religions include the Baha'I Faith, Jainism, Shintoism, Taoism, Tenrikyo, Wicca, and Zoroastrainism. (Pew Research Center)

Protestant–A person who follows the monotheistic religion of Christianity that is not part of Catholic or Eastern Orthodox faith. Members of this faith affirm the Reformation principles of justification by faith alone, the priesthood of all believers, and the primacy of the Bible as the only source of revealed truth. Moreover, believers deny the universal authority of the Pope and some churches are governed by federated councils on the local, national, and international levels. (Merriam-Webster Collegiate Dictionary [Eleventh

Edition, 2003]; the Encyclopedia Britannica Micropedia Ready Reference [15th Edition, 2010])

Sikh–A person who follows the monotheistic religion founded by Guru Nanak in the Punjab region of South Asia. Sikhs follow the teachings of 10 gurus; study from the religion's primary sacred text (i.e., the Guru Granth Sahib), and worship in Gurdwaras. Some members of the Sikh faith may be distinguished by the *dastaar* (Sikh turban) and five religious articles: *kesh* (unshorn hair, including a beard), *kanga* (wooden comb), *kara* (steel bracelet), *kachera* (short trousers), and *kirpan* (religious sword). (Merriam-Webster Collegiate Dictionary [Eleventh Edition, 2003]; the Encyclopedia Britannica Micropedia Ready Reference [15th Edition, 2010])

3.7. Sexual-Orientation Bias and Associated Terms

Sexual-Orientation Bias–(noun) A preformed negative opinion or attitude toward a person or group of persons based on their actual or perceived sexual orientation.

Sexual Orientation–(noun) The term for a person's physical, romantic, and/or emotional attraction to members of the same and/or opposite sex, including lesbian, gay, bisexual, and heterosexual (straight) individuals.

Note: The terms "sexual preference" or "lifestyle" are considered offensive by many members of the lesbian, gay, or bisexual communities.

Bisexual–(adjective) Of or relating to people who are physically, romantically, and/or emotionally attracted to both men and women.

Gay–(adjective) Of or relating to people who are physically, romantically, and/or emotionally attracted to people of the same sex.

> **Note:** Generally this word is used to refer to gay men, but may also be used to describe women; the term "gay" is preferred over the term "homosexual." For FBI UCR Program purposes, however, if reporting an anti-gay bias, the victim should be a male.

Heterosexual–(adjective) Of or relating to people who are physically, romantically, and/or emotionally attracted to people of the opposite sex.

Note: The term "straight" is a synonym.

Homosexual–(adjective) Of or relating to people who are physically, romantically, and/or emotionally attracted to people of the same sex.

Note: This is an outdated clinical term considered derogatory and offensive by many people; current journalistic standards restrict usage of the term; "lesbian" and/or "gay" accurately describes those who are attracted to people of the same sex.

Lesbian–(adjective) Of or relating to women who are physically, romantically, and/or emotionally attracted to other women.

Note: Some lesbian women prefer to be described as gay women; preferred over the term "homosexual;" may be used as a noun. For FBI UCR Program purposes, however, if reporting an anti-gay bias, the victim should be a male.

LGBT–(noun) Common initialism for "lesbian, gay, bisexual, and transgender," used here to refer to community organizations or events that serve lesbian, gay, bisexual, transgender, and allied people.

4. Scenarios of Bias Motivation

The following scenarios offer guidance on how to report hate crime. Based on the facts available, explanations after each scenario provide, as applicable, the known offense(s) and the bias type(s) that law enforcement would report. The number of victims has been added to some of the incidents for clarification purposes.

A. A group home for persons with psychiatric disabilities who were in transition back into the community was the site of a reported arson. Investigation revealed that neighbors had expressed many concerns about the group home in town meetings and were angry that the house was located in their community. Shortly before the fire was reported, a witness heard a man state, "I'll get rid of those 'crazies,' I'll burn them out." Twelve persons, including patients and staff, suffered second and third degree burns.

Offenses–Aggravated Assault (12 victims) and Arson (1 arson). An Anti-Mental Disability Bias should be reported with this incident since the suspect apparently committed the crime due to his bias against persons with psychiatric disabilities.

B. Someone threw a rock breaking a window in a Syrian-owned convenience store. The store had signs written in Arabic displayed in the window and outside the store. The rock, which had a disparaging message about the owner's Arab ancestry, struck the owner in the head, which caused a gash requiring medical attention.

Offenses–Aggravated Assault and Destruction/Damage/Vandalism of Property. This incident should be reported with an Anti-Arab Race/Ethnicity/Ancestry Bias since the evidence indicates the victim was targeted due to his ancestral descent.

C. In a parking lot next to a bar, a 29-year-old Japanese American male was attacked by a 51-year-old white male wielding a tire iron. The victim suffered severe lacerations and a broken arm. Investigation revealed that the offender and victim had previously exchanged racial insults in the bar. The offender initiated the exchange by calling the victim by a well-known and recognized epithet used against the Japanese and complained that the Japanese were taking away jobs from Americans.

Offense–Aggravated Assault. An Anti-Asian Racial Bias should be reported with this incident based on the difference in race of the victim and offender, the exchange of racial insults, and the absence of other reasons for the attack.

D. A street gang assaulted three Hindu men while shouting a well-known Hindu epithet. The gang beat them so severely each suffered a coma.

Offense–Aggravated Assault (3 victims). This incident should be reported with an Anti-Hindu Religious Bias because the evidence indicates the victims were targeted due to their religious affiliation.

E. A woman took a handgun into a fitness center, entered the men's locker room, and fired numerous shots. Two men were killed and one other man was injured in the shooting. The killer's blog revealed that she had planned the attack for some time and harbored a deep hatred for men for rejecting her all of her life.

Offense–Murder (2 victims) and Aggravated Assault (1 victim). This incident should be reported with an Anti-Male Gender Bias because the evidence indicated that the offender harbored a deep hatred for men for rejecting her all of her life.

F. Late in the night, a group of individuals broke in to a local Lesbian, Gay, Bisexual, and Transgender (LGBT) Center. The group painted well-known and recognized LGBT epithets on the walls and stole the gay pride rainbow flag that was flown above the front door of the center.

Offenses–Burglary and Destruction/Damage/Vandalism of Property. This incident should be reported with an Anti-Lesbian, Gay, Bisexual, or Transgender (Mixed Group) Sexual- Orientation Bias based on the offender's intent; the property crime was clearly meant to intimidate the employees and patrons of the center.

G. Two Palestinian university students speaking in Arabic were attending a department reception when another student, a white male, deliberately bumped into one of them. When one Palestinian student said, "Hey, watch where you're going," the white student responded by saying, "I'll go wherever I want. This is my country, **you Arab!**" The aggressor proceeded to punch the Palestinian student in the face.

Offense–Simple Assault. This incident should be reported as Anti-Arab Race/Ethnicity/Ancestry Bias since the evidence indicates the victim was targeted due to his ancestral descent.

H. Overnight, unknown persons broke into a synagogue and destroyed several priceless religious objects. The perpetrators drew a large swastika on the door and wrote "Death to Jews" on a wall. Although other valuable items were present, none were stolen.

Offenses–Burglary and Destruction/Damage/Vandalism of Property. This incident should be reported with an Anti-Jewish Religious Bias because the offenders destroyed priceless religious objects and left anti-Semitic words and graffiti behind, and theft did not appear to be the motive for the burglary.

I. A transgender woman was walking down the street near her home when three men walking toward her said, "Hey, what's your problem? Huh?" She kept walking, trying to ignore them. However, as they got close, one yelled "We don't want no queers in this neighborhood!" and a second one knocked her to the ground.

Offense–Simple Assault. An anti-gay slur was used during this attack because this term was more familiar to the assailants and similar terms are often used interchangeably when referring to anti-gay or anti-transgender/gender nonconforming persons. This incident should be reported with an Anti-Transgender Gender Identity Bias because the victim was attacked for presenting as a female despite having been born biologically male.

J. A female doctor at a small hospital found graffiti scratched into her car. The words were illegible. An investigation revealed that the scratches were deliberately made, but there were no witnesses or suspects. Although she was the only female doctor at the hospital, there were many female nurses who were not targeted, but that fact alone was not sufficient to determine motive or whether the incident should be reported as bias-motivated. However, a month later, two adult males were arrested after being caught on tape vandalizing the female doctor's car again. They admitted to all the incidents, and said that women did not belong in the medical profession.

Offense–Destruction/Damage/Vandalism of Property. In addition to the most recent incident being reported with an Anti-Female Gender Bias, the original incident should also be reported with an Anti-Female Gender Bias because the men's stereotypes about the appropriate gender roles for women prompted their criminal actions in both incidents.

K. An assailant ran by a Sikh pedestrian, shoved him to the ground, forcibly pulled his Dastaar (Sikh turban) and said, "Take that thing off your head–we don't want your kind in this neighborhood!" In the process of the attack, the victim suffered a concussion. When law enforcement responded to the scene, a witness to the attack recognized the offender as a clerk at a local convenience store near a predominantly Sikh community.

Offense–Aggravated Assault. This incident should be reported with an Anti-Sikh Religious Bias because the evidence indicates the victim was targeted due to his Dastaar and the assailant's ongoing dealings with the Sikh community.

L. As a woman entered a local hardware store, she heard someone yell, "Hey there lady, you wanna be a man? You look like a man." She was wearing painting coveralls and had short hair. After making her purchase, she left the store only to see the same individual that had yelled at her slashing her tires. The man fled the scene after spotting her coming out of the store.

Offense–Destruction/Damage/Vandalism of Property. An Anti-Gender Nonconforming Gender-Identity Bias should be reported with this incident since the issue was her clothing and haircut.

M. Six black men assaulted and seriously injured a white man and his Asian male friend as they were walking through a residential neighborhood. Witnesses stated the victims were attacked because they were trespassing in a "black" neighborhood.

Offense–Aggravated Assault (2 victims). An Anti-Multiple Race, Group Racial Bias should be reported with the incident because the victims and offenders were of different races, and witnesses reported that the victims were attacked due to the fact they were not Black or African American.

N. A vandal defaced a Gurdwara (Sikh House of Worship) with graffiti using well-known and recognized Sikh epithets.
Offense–Destruction/Damage/Vandalism of Property. This incident should be reported with an Anti-Sikh Religious Bias because the evidence indicates the Gurdwara and its congregants were targeted because of their religious affiliation.

O. Five gay, male friends, some of whom were wearing makeup and jewelry, were exiting a well-known gay bar when they were approached by a group of men who were unknown to them. The men began to ridicule the gay men's feminine appearance and shouted "Sissy!" "Girlie-men!" and other slurs at them then escalated to physically attacking the victims, rendering them unconscious.
Offense–Aggravated Assault (5 victims). This incident should be reported with an Anti-Gay Sexual-Orientation Bias and an Anti-Gender Nonconforming Gender-Identity Bias because the perpetrators viewed some of the victims as inappropriately crossing gender lines.

P. Overnight, an auditorium used by representatives of several religious denominations to hold an ecumenical conference was vandalized by unknown persons. There was extensive damage to the exterior walls of the building where statements such as "There is but one true religion!" and "Down with the nonbelievers!" were spray painted on them.
Offense–Destruction/Damage/Vandalism of Property. The incident should be reported with an Anti-Multiple Religions, Group Religious Bias because the offenders clearly evidenced their hostility against a group representing more than one religion.

Q. A transgender woman was waiting at a bus stop when she was approached by a man with a history of violent assaults and a previous hate crime conviction. The man physically assaulted the victim, breaking her arm, and then called her a "she-male" and other slurs. The police confirmed that the victim had been simply waiting at the bus stop and the assault was completely unprovoked.

Offense–Aggravated Assault. An Anti-Transgender Gender-Identity Bias should be reported with this incident because the victim was selected solely because of her gender identity and the assailant used an anti-transgender slur during the assault.

R. A man entered a community college and shot and killed a female in a corridor. He then entered a classroom with 10 women and 48 men, fired a shot into the ceiling and said, "I want the women! I hate feminists!" He sent all of the men from the room, lined the women up against the wall and opened fire, killing 6 of the women and wounding the others.

Offenses–Murder (7 victims) and Aggravated Assault (4 victims). This incident should be reported with an Anti-Female Gender Bias because the offender said, "I want the women! I hate feminists!" He also removed all of the men and shot only the women.

S. An African-American man had just finished a midnight riverboat cruise with his fiancée and friends when he escorted his blind, male friend by the arm into a restroom while holding his girlfriends' purse. Inside the restroom, another man shouted anti-black and anti-gay insults at the men. The perpetrator followed them out of the restroom, continuing his verbal harassment. He then went to his car, retrieved a gun, returned to confront the men and said, "Now what have you got to say?" The perpetrator fired the gun killing one of the men.

Offenses–Murder (1 victim) and Aggravated Assault (1 victim). This incident should be reported with an Anti-Black African American Racial Bias and Anti-Gay (Male) Sexual- Orientation Bias because the perpetrator used exclusively anti-black and anti-gay slurs and also acted out on his mistaken perception that the victim was gay.

T. On a cold morning, two Latino immigrant brothers huddled together to stay warm as they walked down the street. Suddenly, two African-American men attacked them. The attackers punched the brothers, causing minor injury, while using anti-gay and anti-Latino slurs. The attackers then fled the scene.

Offense–Simple Assault. This incident should be reported with an Anti-Gay (Male) Sexual- Orientation Bias and Anti-Hispanic or Latino Race/Ethnicity/Ancestry Bias because the perpetrators were motivated by the perceived sexual orientation and race/ethnicity of the brothers, as evidenced by the use of both anti-gay and anti-Latino slurs.

U. An Egyptian-American high school student was on his way to meet friends to play basketball when he was attacked by a gang. The gang chased him, shouting anti-Arab curses and threats. The student ran to a parked taxi nearby, opened the door and slid inside. However, the gang caught hold of him and pulled him outside before the taxi could depart. While gang members held the victim down, one attacker rammed a broomstick into his left eye, gouging it out.

Offense–Aggravated Assault. This bias-motivated incident should be reported with an Anti-Arab Race/Ethnicity/Ancestry Bias since the evidence indicates the victim was targeted due to his ancestral descent.

V. A man wearing a "talik" (a sacred Hindu mark worn on the forehead) was assaulted by two men with baseball bats. During the assault, the men screamed at the victim to "clean that off his head." When taken into custody, the men reported they committed the assault because they want the Hindu people to go back where they came from.

Offense–Aggravated Assault. This incident should be reported as an Anti-Hindu Religious Bias because the evidence indicates the motivation of the attack was due to the victim's religious symbols (the talik) and the offenders' derogatory comments about the Hindu community.

W. A man threw a bomb into a vacant Hindu temple. Following his arrest the next day, the perpetrator told the police of his "dislike of Muslims, Arabs, and Hindus."

Offense–Arson. This incident should be reported as Anti-Hindu Religious Bias because the evidence indicates the temple was targeted because of its affiliation with the Hindu faith.

X. One teen walked up to a Sikh teen in the school hallway and said, "I'm going to cut your hair! The Sikh teen replied, "For what? It is against my religion to cut my hair!" The assailant replied, "I don't care," and later snuck up behind the Sikh teen and cut the victim's hair.

Offense–Simple Assault. This incident should be reported as Anti-Sikh Religious Bias since the evidence indicates the victim was targeted because of his kesh *(unshorn hair).*

Y. An adult white male was approached by four white teenagers who requested money for the bus. When the man refused, one of the youths said to the others, "Let's teach this [epithet for a gay person] a lesson." The victim was punched in the face, knocked to the ground, kicked several times, and robbed of his wristwatch, ring, and wallet. When he reported the crime, the victim advised he did not know the offenders and that he was not gay.

Offense–Robbery. The facts are ambiguous. Although an epithet for a gay person was used by one of the offenders, the victim was not gay. Such epithets are sometimes used as general insults regardless of the targeted person's sexual orientation, and in this case the offenders' motivation appeared to be limited to obtaining money from the victim. Therefore, the incident should not be designated as bias-motivated unless the investigation positively concludes that the offenders' bias was a contributing factor in the crime.*

Z. A white juvenile male snatched a Jewish woman's purse, and in doing so, knocked her down and called her by a well-known and recognized epithet used against Jews. The offender's identity is not known. Although the offender used an epithet for Jews, it is not known whether he belongs to another religious group or whether his motive was anything more than robbery.

Offense–Robbery. Because the facts are ambiguous, agencies should not report this incident as bias-motivated unless the investigation positively concludes that the offender's bias was a contributing factor in the crime.*

***Note:** If the facts are ambiguous, (i.e., where some facts are present but are not conclusive), it is only in the National Incident-Based Reporting System (NIBRS) that incidents involving ambiguous facts can be reported, (i.e., submitted via data value 99 = Unknown in Data Element 8A, Bias Motivation). The intent of bias motivation code 99 = Unknown is to allow a NIBRS agency to report a crime in which bias motivation is unknown or when the investigation has not been completed. If the presence of bias motivation is determined, the reported bias motivation code 99 = Unknown should be modified to indicate the results of the subsequent investigation. Law enforcement agencies should be diligent in modifying these types of situations as they become known. In addition, a law enforcement agency not reporting hate crime in the NIBRS would not submit a Hate Crime Incident Report unless the investigation determined a bias crime did occur.

5. Submitting Hate Crime Data to the FBI UCR Program

Although all hate crime submissions forwarded to the FBI Uniform Crime Reporting (UCR) Program are made electronically, the specific reporting method used depends upon whether a law enforcement agency submits the rest of its UCR data via the National Incident-Based Reporting System (NIBRS) or the Summary Reporting System (SRS). NIBRS agencies report hate crime as part of their regular UCR submission, and SRS agencies use either a separate record layout or a Microsoft Excel worksheet to submit their hate crime data to the UCR Program. All three submission types capture the data required for hate crime—the offense type and its respective bias motivation, the location of the incident, the number and type of victims, the number of known offenders, the known offender's race and ethnicity, and whether or not the victim and/or offender were under 18 years of age and /or 18 years of age and over. However, the offenses that are submitted must be reported in accordance with the requirements of the NIBRS or the SRS, depending on which system is applicable.

5.1. Agencies that Submit Hate Crime Data via the NIBRS

NIBRS participants use Data Element 8A, Bias Motivation, as a mandatory data element with their electronic submissions to indicate whether or not any offenses within reported incidents involved a bias motivation. In addition to capturing the data required for hate crime, these law enforcement agencies can report considerably more information about a hate crime incident because NIBRS is a comprehensive data collection. With the flexibility of NIBRS' rich data, other data elements and codes can be used as needed to comply with revised reporting requirements. More information about how to report data via the NIBRS is provided in the *NIBRS Technical Specification,* which is available at www.fbi.gov/about-us/cjis/ucr/nibrs.

5.1.1. NIBRS Offenses for Which Data Element 8A, Bias Motivation, Is Applicable

The data element that indicates bias motivation of an offense applies to all NIBRS Group A offenses, which are listed below. (The Offense Categories and the UCR Offense Codes for the NIBRS are also included.)

Table 2. NIBRS Offenses for Which Data Element 8A, Bias Motivation, Is Applicable

Offense Category	UCR Code	Offense
	200	Arson
Assault Offenses	13A	Aggravated Assault
	13B	Simple Assault
	13C	Intimidation
	510	Bribery
	220	Burglary/Breaking and Entering
	250	Counterfeiting/Forgery
	290	Destruction/Damage/Vandalism of Property
Drug/Narcotic Offenses	35A	Drug/Narcotic Violations
	35B	Drug/Equipment Violations
	270	Embezzlement
	210	Extortion/Blackmail
Fraud Offenses	26A	False Pretenses/Swindle/Confidence Game
	26B	Credit Card/Automated Teller Machine Fraud
	26C	Impersonation
	26D	Welfare Fraud
	26E	Wire Fraud
Gambling Offenses	39A	Betting/Wagering
	39B	Operating/Promoting/Assisting Gambling
	39C	Gambling Equipment Violations
	39D	Sports Tampering
Homicide Offenses	09A	Murder and Nonnegligent Manslaughter
	09B	Negligent Manslaughter
Human Trafficking Offenses	64A	Commercial Sex Acts
	64B	Involuntary Servitude
	100	Kidnapping/Abduction
Larceny-Theft Offenses	23A	Pocket-picking
	23B	Purse-snatching
	23C	Shoplifting
	23D	Theft From Building
	23E	Theft From Coin-Operated Machine or Device
	23F	Theft From Motor Vehicle
	23G	Theft of Motor Vehicle Parts or Accessories
	23H	All Other Larceny
	240	Motor Vehicle Theft
	370	Pornography/Obscene Material
Prostitution Offenses	40A	Prostitution
	40B	Assisting or Promoting Prostitution

Table 2. (Continued)

Offense Category	UCR Code	Offense
	40C	Purchasing Prostitution
	120	Robbery
Sex Offenses	11A	Rape
	11B	Sodomy
	11C	Sexual Assault With An Object
	11D	Fondling
	36A	Incest
	36B	Statutory Rape
	280	Stolen Property Offenses
	520	Weapon Law Violations

The definitions of these offenses for can be found in Appendix B. Information concerning mutually exclusive and lesser included offenses is also available in that appendix.

5.1.2. NIBRS Data Element 8A, Bias Motivation

This data element, required at the end of the Offense Segment of all NIBRS submissions, indicates whether the offender was motivated, in whole or in part, to commit the offense because of his or her bias against a race, religion, disability, sexual orientation, ethnicity, gender, or gender identity. Due to the difficulty of ascertaining the offender's subjective motivation, bias is to be reported *only if* investigation reveals sufficient objective facts to lead a reasonable and prudent person to conclude that the offender's actions were motivated, in whole or in part, by bias. Refer to Table 1 for the list of bias motivations collected within the FBI's Hate Crime Data Collection.

Table 3. Additional Bias Motivations Collected in NIBRS

Bias Category	Bias Motivation
None/ Unknown	None (No Bias) (88)
	Unknown (Offender's Motivation Not Known) (99)

Note: In the NIBRS, incidents that do not involve any facts indicating bias motivation on the part of the offender are to be coded as 88 = None, and incidents involving ambiguous facts (i.e., where some facts are present but are not conclusive) should be coded as 99 = Unknown. The intent of bias motivation code 99 = Unknown is to allow an agency to report a crime in which bias motivation is unknown or when the investigation has not been completed. When it is determined the presence of bias motivation is conclusive, the reported bias motivation code 99 = Unknown should be modified to indicate the results of the subsequent investigation. Law enforcement agencies should be diligent in modifying these types of situations as they become known. A review of year-end hate crime data should have few, if any, hate crimes coded as 99 = Unknown.

5.2. Agencies that Submit Hate Crime Data via the SRS

5.2.1. Methods for SRS Agencies to Submit Hate Crime Data

Agencies not yet participating in the NIBRS submit their hate crime data electronically via Microsoft Excel worksheets or via a hate crime record layout.

A. Agencies may submit the Hate Crime Incident Report via a Microsoft Excel worksheet as part of their regular SRS submissions.
B. State UCR Programs can include a hate crime record layout as part of their regular SRS submissions. The hate crime data submission specifications are provided in *Hate Crime Technical Specification*, which is available at <www.fbi.gov/aboutus/cjis/ucr/technical-specifications>.

5.2.2. Offenses for Which Hate Crime Reporting Is Applicable for SRS Agencies

SRS agencies should use the hate crime record layout or the Microsoft Excel worksheet to report the following offense categories:

Table 4. Offenses for Which Hate Crime Reporting is Applicable for SRS Agencies

UCR Offense Codes	Offenses
01	Murder and Nonnegligent Manslaughter
02	Rape/Sodomy/Sexual Assault With An Object
03	Robbery
04	Aggravated Assault
05	Burglary
06	Larceny-Theft

Table 4. (Continued)

UCR Offense Codes	Offenses
07	Motor Vehicle Theft
08	Arson
09	Simple Assault
10	Intimidation
11	Destruction/Damage/Vandalism of Property
12	Human Trafficking-Commercial Sex Acts
13	Human Trafficking-Involuntary Servitude

The definitions of these offenses for reporting hate crime on the hate crime record layout or the Microsoft Excel worksheet can be found in Appendix B. Information concerning mutually exclusive and lesser included offenses is also available in that appendix.

5.2.3. Additional Instructions for SRS Agencies

The following additional instructions are applicable to law enforcement agencies that submit hate crime data through either the hate crime record layout or the Microsoft Excel worksheet.

Simple Assault and Intimidation–In the SRS, Simple Assault and Intimidation are not reported separately. Both are reported on the Return A—Monthly Return of Offenses Known to the Police form as Other Assaults-Simple, Not Aggravated. However, for the purpose of hate crime reporting, SRS agencies should report Simple Assault and Intimidation separately using the definitions found in Appendix B.

Destruction/Damage/Vandalism of Property–In the SRS, Vandalism is reported on the Age, Sex, Race, and Ethnicity of Persons Arrested form only when arrests occur. Likewise, destruction and damage of property, which may be reported as either Vandalism or All Other Offenses depending on the facts of the case, are reported only when arrests occur. However, for the purpose of hate crime reporting, all three offenses fall into the category of Destruction/Damage/Vandalism of Property and should be reported regardless of whether arrests have taken place. The offense is defined in Appendix B.

Nonapplicability of the Hierarchy Rule–In the SRS under the Hierarchy Rule, only the most serious Part I offense in a multiple-offense incident is to be reported. However, for hate crime reporting purposes, all of the above-mentioned offenses which were identified as bias motivated and occurred during the incident should be reported.

UCR Offense and Code Segment–The number of victims involved in each offense for which bias/hate motivation has been determined should be listed. When Individual is reported as the Victim Type, the Total Number of Victims, Total Number of Victims 18 and over, and Total Number of Victims under 18 must also be reported. Similar information on the offender, if known, is collected.

Multiple Offense Incidents–In the event of multiple offense codes and victims, only those for which bias/hate motivation exists should be listed. **Do not** list an offense code and its victims when the motivation is clearly not based on bias or when the motivation is unknown.

> For example, a robbery occurred at a bar and its patrons were robbed by two offenders. During the robbery, a female Asian patron was raped by one of the offenders. Subsequent investigation reveals that while the robbery motive did not involve bias, the rape was bias motivated. Therefore, only the rape should be reported as a hate crime.

Updating–For updating purposes, a copy of the report should be retained by the agency. Corrections/updates should be accomplished by selecting the "Adjustment box" within the Microsoft Excel worksheet and providing the appropriate changes or by sending an adjusted record in the hate crime record layout. Incidents can be deleted by simply selecting the "Delete box" within the Microsoft Excel worksheet, or by specifying a "D" in the record type field within the hate crime record layout; leave the ORI Number and Incident Number, then delete all of the remaining data.

6. Learning Modules for Recognizing and Reporting Hate Crimes

6.1. Use of the Enclosed Learning Modules

The FBI Uniform Crime Reporting (UCR) Program has included two learning modules within this manual for use in the instruction of law enforcement personnel on hate crime matters. The modules are in no way exhaustive or exclusive of either what can be trained or the way the material should be presented. Rather, they are intended merely as a suggested approach to such instruction. In order to obtain the most benefit from the materials, an agency should tailor them to meet its unique needs. The reader may also be interested in the model training programs produced by the International Association of Chiefs of Police (IACP) and the National Organization of Black Law Enforcement Executives (NOBLE). This training information can be obtained by contacting the organizations directly.

6.1.1. Overview of Learning Module One

"Learning Module One: Hate Crime Reporting Model: The Two-Tier Decision Making Process" includes a hate crime reporting model that can be adapted for law enforcement use. Refer to Section 3 of this manual for the entire list of bias definitions law enforcement officers need to know in dealing with hate crime.

The most important aspect of the model concerns the two-tier reviewing process. The purpose of the two-tier procedure is to ensure that suspected bias-motivated incidents undergo two levels of review within the reporting agency. Under the model system, the officer who responds to the incident is responsible for determining whether there is any indication that the offender was motivated by bias. If so, the responding officer should designate the incident as a "Suspected Bias-Motivated Crime" and pass it on for review by a second officer (or unit) possessing greater expertise in hate crime matters. This latter officer or unit has the responsibility for making the final decision as to whether the incident constitutes a hate crime. It is only after the incident has undergone the second review and is determined to be a hate crime that it is ready to be reported as such to the FBI UCR Program.

6.1.2. Overview of Learning Module Two

"Learning Module Two: Case Study Exercises of Possible Bias-Related Crimes" gives the student officer the opportunity to apply his or her newly-gained knowledge of hate crime matters to hypothetical cases. The student is to read each case scenario and (1) classify the type of offense(s) involved in the incident, (2) classify the offense as either "Not a Bias-Motivated Crime" or a "Suspected Bias-Motivated Crime," and (3) provide reasons for his or her decisions.

6.2. Learning Module One: Hate Crime Reporting Model: The Two-Tier Decision Making Process

6.2.1. Module Description

This module provides: (1) definitions of hate crime terminology, (2) a "model" approach to reporting hate crimes, and (3) criteria for determining whether a hate crime has occurred.

6.2.2. Course Objectives

- The student will be able to define Bias/Hate Crime based on race, religion, disability, sexual orientation, ethnicity, gender, and gender identity, as well as Responding Officer, and Second-Level Judgment Officer/Unit.
- The student will be able to explain the "two-tier" process for reporting hate crimes.
- The student will be able to list the types of criteria used to make a determination of whether a crime was bias motivated.

6.2.3. Definitions for Hate Crime Data Collection:

The following is an abbreviated list of definitions that have been adopted for use in hate crime reporting (See Section 3 for the entire list of bias definitions):

Bias–A preformed negative opinion or attitude toward a group of persons based on their race, religion, disability, sexual orientation, ethnicity, gender, or gender identity.

Bias Crime—A committed criminal offense that is motivated, in whole or in part, by the offender's bias(es) against a race, religion, disability, sexual orientation, ethnicity, gender, or gender identity; also known as Hate Crime.

> **Note:** Even if the offender was mistaken in his or her perception that the victim was a member of the group he or she was acting against, the offense is still a bias crime because the offender was motivated by bias against the group.

Disability Bias–A preformed negative opinion or attitude toward a group of persons based on their physical or mental impairments, whether such disability is temporary or permanent, congenital or acquired by heredity, accident, injury, advanced age, or illness.

Gender Bias–(noun) A preformed negative opinion or attitude toward a person or group of persons based on their actual or perceived gender, i.e., male or female.

Gender Identity Bias–A preformed negative opinion or attitude toward a person or group of persons based on their actual or perceived gender identity, e.g., bias against transgender or gender nonconforming individuals.

Hate Crime–Bias Crime.

Hate Group–An organization whose primary purpose is to promote animosity, hostility, and malice against persons of or with a race, religion, disability, sexual orientation, ethnicity, gender, or gender identity which differs from that of the members or the organization, e.g., the Ku Klux Klan, American Nazi Party.

Race/Ethnicity/Ancestry Bias

Note: When the FBI's Hate Crime Statistics Program was initially implemented, racial bias was reported as a separate category and ethnicity bias was reported as ethnicity/national origin bias. It was then modified by the Office of Management and Budget's (OMB's) *1997 Revision to the Standards for the Classification of Federal Data on Race and Ethnicity.* With the revised race and ethnicity categories and the addition of an ancestry (a subcategory of ethnicity), the OMB advised the program to publish the data in the combined category of Race/Ethnicity/Ancestry Bias.

Racial Bias–A preformed negative opinion or attitude toward a group of persons who possess common physical characteristics, e.g., color of skin, eyes, and/or hair, facial features, etc., genetically transmitted by descent and heredity which distinguish them as a distinct division of humankind, e.g., Asians, Blacks or African Americans, whites.

Ethnicity Bias–A preformed negative opinion or attitude toward a group of people whose members identify with each other, through a common heritage, often consisting of a common language, common culture (often including a shared religion) and/or ideology that stresses common ancestry. The concept of ethnicity differs from the closely related term *race* in that "race" refers to grouping based mostly upon biological criteria, while "ethnicity" also encompasses additional cultural factors.

Ancestry Bias–A preformed negative opinion or attitude toward a group of people based on their common lineage or descent.

Religious Bias–A preformed negative opinion or attitude toward a group of persons who share the same religious beliefs regarding the origin and purpose of the universe and the existence or nonexistence of a supreme being, e.g., Catholics, Jews, Protestants, atheists.

Sexual-Orientation Bias–(noun) A preformed negative opinion or attitude toward a person or group of persons based on their actual or perceived sexual orientation.

6.2.4. Procedures and Criteria

6.2.4.1. Two-Tier Decision-Making Process

The FBI UCR Program surveyed state UCR Program managers on hate crime collection procedures in use at various law enforcement agencies within their states. It found that most law enforcement agencies that collect hate crime data employ a two-tier decision-making process. The first level is the law enforcement officer who initially responds to the alleged hate crime incident, i.e., the "responding officer" (or "first-level judgment officer"). It is the responsibility of the responding officer to determine whether there is any indication that the offender was motivated by bias. If there is, the officer is to designate the incident as a "suspected bias-motivated crime" and forward the case file to a "second-level judgment officer/unit." In smaller agencies this is usually a person specially trained in hate crime matters, while in larger agencies it may be a special unit.

It is the task of the second-level judgment officer/unit to review carefully the facts of the incident and make the final determination of whether a hate crime has actually occurred. If so, the incident is to be reported to the FBI UCR Program as a bias-motivated crime.

6.2.4.2. Responding Officer's Responsibilities

Law enforcement's response to an alleged hate crime begins no different than to any other crime. The Responding Officer must quickly evaluate wh has happened and take any necessary action to stabilize the situation. A that has been done, there are two unique areas of concern which shoul recognized by an officer responding to an alleged hate crime: (1) sensitivi the needs of the victim and (2) the elements of a bias crime.

First, the responding officer should be sensitive to the effects of crime on the victim. A victim of any crime may feel isolated from fearful that the occurrence will happen again, and angry that he or become a victim. However, there is a deeper level of isolation, fear, a that the victim of hate crime feels. This individual has been chosen from the rest of the population to be victimized for no other reason than his or her race, religion, disability, sexual orientation, ethnicity, gender, or gender identity. There is nothing this person can do; indeed, there is nothing he or she ought to do to change his or her race, religion, disability, sexual orientation, ethnicity, gender, and gender identity. And yet, it is because of these very innate qualities that he or she was victimized. This type of personal experience can result, many times, in a feeling of loss of control over one's life. By recognizing these dynamics, the responding officer can address the special needs of the victim, thereby placing him or her at some ease and thereby making it easier to elicit from him or her necessary information concerning the alleged offense. Another task of the responding officer is to determine whether additional resources are needed on the scene, such as community affairs/relations representatives, mental/physical health professionals, and/or the clergy. At a minimum, the victim should be referred to appropriate social and legal services.

Second, the responding officer must be knowledgeable of the elements of a bias-related crime. As set forth in this document, a bias crime is a criminal offense committed against a person or property or if reported in the NIBRS, a crime against society (i.e., Drug/Narcotic Offenses, Gambling Offenses, Pornography/Obscene Material, Prostitution Offenses, and Weapon Law Violations), which is motivated by the offender's bias against the victim's race, religion, disability sexual orientation, ethnicity, gender, or gender identity. At the level of the responding officer, if there is any indication that the offender was motivated by bias to commit the crime, the incident should be classified as a "suspected bias-motivated crime."

The types of factors to be considered by the reporting officer in making a determination of whether the incident is a "suspected bias-motivated crime" are:

- Is the motivation of the alleged offender known?
- Was the incident known to have been motivated by racial, religious, disability, sexual orientation, ethnic, gender, or gender identity bias?
- Does the victim perceive the action of the offender to have been motivated by bias?
- Is there no clear other motivation for the incident?
- Were any racial, religious, disability, sexual orientation, ethnic, gender, or gender identity bias remarks made by the offender?

- Were there any offensive symbols, words, or acts which are known to represent a hate group or other evidence of bias against the victim's group?
- Did the incident occur on a holiday or other day of significance to the victim's or offender's group?
- What do the demographics of the area tell you about the incident?

If these or other factors indicate that the offender may have been motivated by bias to commit the crime, the incident should be classified as a "suspected bias-motivated crime" and sent on to the second-level judgment officer/unit for review. While the mere utterance of a racial epithet by the offender does not provide sufficient basis to report a crime as a "suspected bias-motivated crime," it, combined with other factors indicating bias, could do so. For the purpose of first-level bias crime reporting, the old adage of "when in doubt, check it out" should be followed, i.e., questionable cases should be referred to the second-level judgment officer/unit for resolution.

6.2.4.3. Second Level Judgment Officer's/Unit's Responsibilities

The second tier in the decision-making process is where the final decision is made regarding whether an offense was bias motivated. Therefore, the people who make final decisions must be specially trained to the point of being "experts" on bias matters. The responding officer had merely to determine whether there was any indication that the offense was motivated by bias. On the other hand, the second-level judgment officer/unit must carefully sift through the facts using more stringent criteria to determine whether the incident was, in fact, a hate crime.

The second level of review can be a specially trained officer, investigator, supervisor, or specially-established hate crime unit. This does not mean that every agency must establish a "special hate crime unit." Given the fiscal constraints prevalent throughout most of the law enforcement community, such a proposition would be an unreasonable requirement. However, what is suggested is that somewhere in the agency's already established crime reporting review process, someone should be specifically tasked with the responsibility of reviewing "suspected bias-motivated crimes" and making the final decision as to the existence or nonexistence of bias motivation.

During the second review, the second-level judgment officer/unit should have time to consider carefully the findings of the responding officer and perhaps even conduct interviews of the victims and witnesses if necessary. For an incident to be reported as a hate crime, sufficient objective facts must be present to lead a reasonable and prudent person to conclude that the offender's actions were motivated, in whole or in part, by bias. While no single fact may be conclusive, positive answers to the types of questions listed below are supportive of a finding of bias motivation. It is important for a distinction to be established. The mere fact that the offender is biased against the victim's race, religion, disability, sexual orientation, ethnicity, gender, and/or gender identity does not mean a hate crime was involved. Rather, the offender's criminal act must have been motivated, in whole or in part, by his or her bias.

The second-level judgment officer/unit should seek answers to the following types of questions before making the final determination of whether an incident was motivated by bias:

- Is the victim a member of a specific race, religion, disability, sexual orientation, ethnicity, gender, or gender identity?
- Was the offender of a different race, religion, sexual orientation, ethnicity, gender, or gender identity than the victim? For example, the victim was African American and the offender was white.
- Would the incident have taken place if the victim and offender were of the same race, religion, disability, sexual orientation, ethnicity, gender, or gender identity?
- Were biased oral comments, written statements, or gestures made by the offender which indicated offender's bias? For example, the offender shouted a racial or ethnic epithet at the victim.
- Were bias-related drawings, markings, symbols, or graffiti left at the crime scene, e.g., a swastika was painted on the door of a synagogue, mosque, or LGBT Center.?
- Were certain objects, items, or things that indicate bias used, e.g., the offenders wore white sheets with hoods covering their faces; a burning cross was left in front of the victim's residence?
- Is the victim a member of a specific group which is overwhelmingly outnumbered by other residents in the neighborhood where the victim lives and the incident took place?
- Was the victim visiting a neighborhood where previous hate crimes had been committed because of race, religion, disability, sexual orientation, ethnicity, gender, or gender identity and where tensions remained high against victim's group?
- Have several incidents occurred in the same locality, at or about the same time, and were the victims all of the same race, religion, disability, sexual orientation, ethnicity, gender, or gender identity?

- Does a substantial portion of the community where the crime occurred perceive that the incident was motivated by bias?
- Was the victim engaged in activities related to his or her race, religion, disability, sexual orientation, ethnicity, gender, or gender identity? For example, the victim was a member of the NAACP or participated in an LGBT Pride celebration.
- Did the incident coincide with a holiday or a date of particular significance relating to a race, religion, disability, sexual orientation, ethnicity, gender, or gender identity, e.g., Martin Luther King Day, Rosh Hashanah, or the Transgender Day of Remembrance?
- Was the offender previously involved in a similar hate crime or is a hate group member?
- Were there indications that a hate group was involved? For example, a hate group claimed responsibility for the crime or was active in the neighborhood.
- Does a historically-established animosity exist between the victim's and offender's groups?
- Is this incident similar to other known and documented cases of bias, particularly in this area? Does it fit a similar modus operandi to these other incidents?
- Has this victim been previously involved in similar situations?
- Are there other explanations for the incident, such as a childish prank, unrelated vandalism, etc.?
- Did the offender have some understanding of the impact his or her actions would have on the victim?

The second-level judgment officer/unit should respond to the scenes of large bias incidents, such as race riots, demonstrations, etc. When doing so, a determination should be made whether additional resources should be called to the scene, such as police tactical units, community affairs/relations representatives, mental/physical health professionals, and faith leaders.

It is important to note that only after the second-level judgment officer/unit has made a decision that the crime was bias motivated should it be reported to the FBI UCR Program.

6.3. Learning Module Two: Case Studies of Potential Bias-Related Crimes

6.3.1. Module Description

This module provides the student officer with hypothetical case scenarios to practice his or her knowledge gained from Learning Module One.

6.3.2. Course Objectives

The student will be able to evaluate a hypothetical case and (1) classify the offenses involved in the incident, (2) classify the incident as either "not a bias-motivated crime" or a "suspected bias-motivated crime," and (3) give the reasons for his or her decision.

6.3.3. Rules for the Exercise Session

The student officer is to read the hypothetical cases and (1) classify the offense(s) involved in each incident, (2) classify the fact situations as either 'not a bias-motivated crime" or a "bias-motivated crime," and (3) give reasons for his or her bias classification decisions.

6.3.4. Case Exercises

Exercise 1: Deputy Sheriff Jackson received a radio call to go to an apartment and interview an individual complaining of threats made over the telephone. Upon arriving at the apartment, the complainant, a white female, informed Deputy Jackson she is a lesbian and that over the last two weeks she has received repeated telephone calls from a person who stated that the complainant had been seen going into "gay bars," and therefore, she would have to be "punished."

> **Crime Classification:** Intimidation Bias Classification: Anti-Lesbian
> **Reasons:** Threats were made to harm the victim physically because of her sexual orientation.

Note: In addition to collecting hate crimes based on gender and gender identity, the Matthew Shepard and James Byrd, Jr. Hate Crimes Prevention Act requires statistics to be captured on hate crimes committed by/directed against juveniles. In Exercise 1, however, it is not possible to report the age of the offender. Therefore, when an agency reports this hate crime incident it should submit one offender and the age breakdown should be entered as 00.

Exercise 2: On January 1, a woman was walking alone after leaving a party when she was tackled to the ground by a man. He began choking her and yelling "I hate you!" "You bitch." Nearby, an-undercover officer heard the man yelling and responded. The officer was able to restrain the man but he continued screaming "I hate all of the bitches." The victim indicated she had never seen the man before. Later the man told the officer he had been at a bar and had tried to talk to a woman. She had laughed at him, and he said he was not going to take it anymore.

Crime Classification: Aggravated Assault
Bias Classification: Anti-Female
Reasons: The offender attacked the woman because of his bias against women. This is evidenced by his statements and also by what he told the officer.

Exercise 3: On February 2, at 3:30 a.m., Detective Phipps came across a vehicle that appeared to be abandoned. When he approached the vehicle, he found an unconscious individual who had sustained several bruises to the head. The individual was partially dressed in women's clothing and was biologically male. The detective noted the word "Tranny," written on the windshield as well as a dress and wig on the passenger seat. In addition, he found a state-issued driver's license in the car that identified the victim as having a female name.

Crime Classification: Aggravated Assault
Bias Classification: Anti-Gender Nonconforming and Anti-Transgender
Reasons: The incident should be reported with an Anti-Gender Non-Conforming Bias and Anti-Transgender Bias because the victim appears to have been targeted for dressing in a way that does not correspond to the victim's; birth sex. Based on the evidence, it is unclear if the victim was attacked for wearing women's clothing and a wig at the time of the attack (anti-gender nonconforming) or for living as a female despite being born biologically male (anti-transgender).

Exercise 4: While on foot patrol, Officer Sloan heard two individuals who were engaged in a shouting match. As the officer approached, she saw two men, one white and the other black, shouting obscenities at each other. The argument concerned a parking space to which each believed he was entitled. As the argument continued, one of the men shouted a racial epithet. Officer

Sloan responded and quieted the men. Apparently the first driver to arrive did not use his turn signal to indicate he was waiting to pull into the parking space. The second driver, coming upon what appeared to be an unoccupied parking space, proceeded to maneuver his car around the first driver's car and into the space. The argument then began.

Crime Classification: None
Bias Classification: Unbiased Crime Incident
Reasons: The argument only involved the issue of which driver deserved to get the parking space. One of the questions one should ask in investigating alleged bias incidents is: "Would the incident have taken place if both the victim and offender were of the same race, religion, sexual orientation, ethnicity, gender, or gender identity? If the answer is "Yes," it is "not a bias-motivated crime."

Exercise 5: During the midnight tour, Deputy Sheriff Hennessey was patrolling her assigned watch area. Shining her cruiser light on various business establishments, she noticed one building had been spray painted. The graffiti included racial epithets used against Asians and threats against the owners of a Chinese restaurant that is located in the building. The deputy knows the Chinese owners are the only Asians in that business district. No other buildings were spray painted.

Crime Classification: Destruction/Damage/Vandalism of Property
Bias Classification: Anti-Asian
Reasons: The offenders apparently were motivated by their bias against Asians. This is evidenced by their use of Asian epithets and the fact that no other business in the area was spray painted.

Exercise 6: At 8:30 p.m., Officer Gregory responded to a report of an altercation at a bar/restaurant. Upon arriving at the scene, he found paramedics providing medical care to an African-American male. The victim informed Officer Gregory he was accosted by three white male patrons who repeatedly asked if he were gay. He politely told the aggressors he was not. Officer Gregory also spoke to the bartender who indicated he had noticed the odd behavior in the men, as they took turns leaving the restaurant to go outside, then returning while another took their place. According to the victim, one of the men approached him when he left the restaurant and hurled racial and gay epithets at him. Then another one of the three men struck the male forcefully in the head. The blow knocked the victim to the pavement where he hit his head, rendering him unconscious.

Crime Classification: Aggravated Assault
Bias Classification: Anti-Black or African American and Anti-Gay (Male)
Reasons: The offenders apparently were motivated by their perception that the man was gay and their bias against African Americans.
Note: Up to five bias motivations per offense type can be reported.

Exercise 7: On July 9, at 10:30 p.m., Officer Cassidy was dispatched to investigate a 911 call. Upon arriving at the location, she found a woman who had been beaten. The victim explained that she had been walking home from an LGBT Center when she was accosted by two men. She stated the men beat her and were also verbally abusive and mocked her for her short hair style and for how masculine her clothes and shoes were.

Crime Classification: Aggravated Assault
Bias Classification: Anti-Gender Nonconforming
Reasons: The perpetrators attacked the victim because she did not fit the image they associated as female.

Exercise 8: At 11 p.m. Officers Reid and Shandler responded to the scene of a reported arson. The target of the arson was a group home for persons with psychiatric disabilities who were in transition back into the community. Investigation revealed that neighbors had expressed many concerns about the group home and were angry that the house was located in their community. Shortly before the fire was reported, a witness heard a male voice state, "I'll get rid of those 'crazies.' I'll burn them out."

Crime Classification: Arson
Bias Classification: Anti-Mental Disability
Reasons: The suspect committed the crime of arson primarily because of his bias against persons with psychiatric disabilities. The witness heard a statement that supports the bias motivation finding.

Exercise 9: While on patrol in his police car, Officer Lopez noticed an individual, who later identified himself as Mr. Chopra, attempting to scrub some painted words and markings off of his car, which was parked outside the apartment building where he lives. Officer Lopez asked Mr. Chopra what happened to his car. Mr. Chopra explained that he had moved into the neighborhood three weeks ago and unknown person(s) had repeatedly painted his car and the door of his apartment with racial slurs targeting Black people. Mr. Chopra said he did not understand why this was happening to him because he is not African American and he had immigrated to the United States from India.

Crime Classification: Destruction/Damage/Vandalism of Property
Bias Classification: Anti-Black or African American
Reasons: Although Mr. Chopra is not African American, it is the perception of the offender(s) that he is a member of a minority against which they are biased. Even when offenders commit a crime based on their mistaken perception of the victim, the offense is still a hate crime because the offenders' actions were motivated by bias.

Exercise 10: Someone threw a rock breaking a window in a Syrian-owned convenience store. The store had signs written in Arabic displayed in the window and outside the store. The rock, which had a disparaging message about the owner's Arab ancestry, struck the owner, Mr. Amari, in the head causing injury.

Crime Classification: Aggravated Assault and Destruction/Damage/Vandalism of Property.
Bias Classification: Anti-Arab Race/Ethnicity/Ancestry
Reasons: The evidence in this incident, signs written in Arabic on the outside of the store and the message on the rock, indicates the victim was targeted due to his ancestral descent.

Exercise 11: An adult assailant ran by Mr. Singh, an elderly Sikh pedestrian, shoved him to the ground, forcibly pulled his Dastaar (Sikh turban), and said, "Take that towel off your head–we don't want your kind in this neighborhood!" In the process of the attack, the victim suffered a concussion. When law enforcement responded to the scene, a witness to the attack recognized the offender as a clerk at a local convenience store near a predominately Sikh community.

Crime Classification: Aggravated Assault
Bias Classification: Anti-Sikh Religious Bias

Reasons: The evidence in the incident indicates the victim was targeted because he was wearing a Dastaar. The facts uncovered in the above referenced investigation (e.g., the assailant had dealings with the Sikh community) indicated the assailant's motivation was directed at the victim because he was Sikh.

Exercise 12: Mr. Malakar, who was wearing a "talik" (a sacred Hindu mark worn on the forehead) was assaulted by two juvenile gang members with baseball bats. During the assault, the two gang members screamed at Mr. Malakar to "clean that off [his] head." When taken into custody, the two juveniles reported they committed the assault because they want the Hindu people to go back where they came from."

Crime Classification: Aggravated Assault
Bias Classification: Anti-Hindu Religious Bias
Reasons: The evidence in this incident, the "talik" on the victim's forehead and the offenders' derogatory comments about the Hindu community, indicate the offender's motivation for the attack was the victim's religion.
Note: Additional scenarios of bias motivations are provided in Section 4.

Appendix A. Legislation

As Amended, 28 U.S.C. § 534

§ "[Sec. 1.] (a) This Act may be cited as the 'Hate Crime Statistics Act'. "(b)

(1) Under the authority of section 534 of title 28, United States Code, the Attorney General shall acquire data, for each calendar year, about crimes that manifest evidence of prejudice based on race, gender and gender identity, religion, disability, sexual orientation, or ethnicity, including where appropriate the crimes of murder, non-negligent manslaughter; forcible rape; aggravated assault, simple assault, intimidation; arson; and destruction, damage or vandalism of property.

"(2) The Attorney General shall establish guidelines for the collection of such data including the necessary evidence and criteria that must be present for a finding of manifest prejudice and procedures for carrying out the purposes of this section.

"(3) Nothing in this section creates a cause of action or a right to bring an action, including an action based on discrimination due to sexual orientation. As used in this section, the term 'sexual orientation' means consensual homosexuality or heterosexuality. This subsection does not limit any existing cause of action or right to bring an action, including any action under the Administrative Procedure Act or the All Writs Act [5 U.S.C.S. §§ 551 et seq. or 28 U.S.C.S. § 1651].

"(4) Data acquired under this section shall be used only for research or statistical purposes and may not contain any information that may reveal the identity of an individual victim of a crime.

"(5) The Attorney General shall publish an annual summary of the data acquired under this section, including data about crimes committed by, and crimes directed against, juveniles.

"(c) There are authorized to be appropriated such sums as may be necessary to carry out the provisions of this section through fiscal year 2002.

"Sec. 2. (a) Congress finds that—

"(1) the American family life is the foundation of American Society,

"(2) Federal policy should encourage the well-being, financial security, and health of the American family,

"(3) schools should not de-emphasize the critical value of American family life.

"(b) Nothing in this Act shall be construed, nor shall any funds appropriated to carry out the purpose of the Act be used, to promote or encourage homosexuality."

Public Law 103-322—Sept. 13, 1994

108 STAT. 2131

Subsection (b) (1) of the first section of the Hate Crime Statistics Act (28 U.S.C. 534 note) is amended by inserting "disability," after "religion,".

Public Law 104-155—July 3, 1996

Subsection (b)(1) of the first section of the Hate Crime Statistics Act (28 U.S.C. 534 note) is amended by striking "for the calendar year 1990 and each succeeding 4 calendar years," and by inserting "for each calendar year."

Public Law 111-84—October 28, 2009

On October 28, 2009, the President signed into law the *Matthew Shepard and James Byrd, Jr. Hate Crimes Prevention Act,* under Division E. P.L. 111-84, the *National Defense Authorization Act for Fiscal Year 2010.* This Act also complements a 1968 United States federal hate-crime law. The new law, 18 U.S.C. §249, includes crimes motivated by a victim's actual or perceived gender, sexual orientation, gender identity, religion, race, color, national origin, or disability. The *Matthew Shepard and James Byrd Jr, Act* specifically states under Sec. 4709. Statistics:

> Subsection (b) (1) of the first section of the Hate Crime Statistics Act (28 U.S.C. 534 note) is amended by inserting "gender and gender identity," after "race;" and
>
> Subsection (b)(5) of the first section of the Hate Crime Statistics Act (28 U.S.C. 534 note) is amended by inserting "including data about crimes committed by, and crimes directed against, juvenile," after "data acquired under this section."

Appendix B. UCR Offense Definitions

B.1. NIBRS Offenses and Definitions

Arson—To unlawfully and intentionally damage, or attempt to damage, any real or personal property by fire or incendiary device.

Assault Offenses—An unlawful attack by one person upon another.

> **Aggravated Assault**—An unlawful attack by one person upon another wherein the offender uses a weapon or displays it in a threatening manner, or the victim suffers obvious severe or aggravated bodily injury involving apparent broken bones, loss of teeth, possible internal injury, severe laceration, or loss of consciousness. This also includes assault with disease (as in cases when the offender is aware that he/she is infected with a deadly disease and deliberately attempts to inflict the disease by biting, spitting, etc.).
>
> **Simple Assault**—An unlawful physical attack by one person upon another where neither the offender displays a weapon, nor the victim

suffers obvious severe or aggravated bodily injury involving apparent broken bones, loss of teeth, possible internal injury, severe laceration, or loss of consciousness.

Intimidation—To unlawfully place another person in reasonable fear of bodily harm through the use of threatening words and/or other conduct, but without displaying a weapon or subjecting the victim to actual physical attack.

Bribery—(Except "Sports Bribery") The offering, giving, receiving, or soliciting of anything of value (i.e., a bribe, gratuity, or kickback) to sway the judgment or action of a person in a position of trust or influence.

Burglary/Breaking and Entering—The unlawful entry into a building or other structure with the intent to commit a felony or a theft.

Counterfeiting/Forgery—The altering, copying, or imitation of something, without authority or right, with the intent to deceive or defraud by passing the copy or thing altered or imitated as that which is original or genuine; or the selling, buying, or possession of an altered, copied, or imitated thing with the intent to deceive or defraud.

Destruction/Damage/Vandalism of Property—(Except "Arson") To willfully or maliciously destroy, damage, deface, or otherwise injure real or personal property without the consent of the owner or the person having custody or control of it.

Drug/Narcotic Offenses—(Except "Driving Under the Influence") The violation of laws prohibiting the production, distribution, and/or use of certain controlled substances and the equipment or devices utilized in their preparation and/or use.

Drug/Narcotic Violations—The unlawful cultivation, manufacture, distribution, sale, purchase, use, possession, transportation, or importation of any controlled drug or narcotic substance.

Drug Equipment Violations—The unlawful manufacture, sale, purchase, possession, or transportation of equipment or devices utilized in preparing and/or using drugs or narcotics.

Embezzlement—The unlawful misappropriation by an offender to his/her own use or purpose of money, property, or some other thing of value entrusted to his/her care, custody, or control.

Extortion/Blackmail—To unlawfully obtain money, property, or any other thing of value, either tangible or intangible, through the use or threat of force, misuse of authority, threat of criminal prosecution, threat of destruction of reputation or social standing, or through other coercive means.

Fraud Offenses—(Except "Counterfeiting/Forgery" and "Bad Checks") The intentional perversion of the truth for the purpose of inducing another person, or other entity, in reliance upon it to part with something of value or to surrender a legal right.

False Pretenses/Swindle/Confidence Game—The intentional misrepresentation of existing fact or condition, or the use of some other deceptive scheme or device, to obtain money, goods, or other things of value.

Credit Card/Automated Teller Machine Fraud—The unlawful use of a credit (or debit) card or automated teller machine for fraudulent purposes.

Impersonation—Falsely representing one's identity or position, and acting in the character or position thus unlawfully assumed, to deceive others and thereby gain a profit or advantage, enjoy some right or privilege, or subject another person or entity to an expense, charge, or liability which would not have otherwise been incurred.

Welfare Fraud—The use of deceitful statements, practices, or devices to unlawfully obtain welfare benefits.

Wire Fraud—The use of an electric or electronic communications facility to intentionally transmit a false and/or deceptive message in furtherance of a fraudulent activity.

Gambling Offenses—To unlawfully bet or wager money or something else of value; assist, promote, or operate a game of chance for money or some other stake; possess or transmit wagering information; manufacture, sell, purchase, possess, or transport gambling equipment, devices or goods; or tamper with the outcome of a sporting event or contest to gain a gambling advantage.

Betting/Wagering—To unlawfully stake money or something else of value on the happening of an uncertain event or on the ascertainment of a fact in dispute.

Operating/Promoting/Assisting Gambling—To unlawfully operate, promote, or assist in the operation of a game of chance, lottery, or other gambling activity.

Gambling Equipment Violations—To unlawfully manufacture, sell, buy, possess, or transport equipment, devices, and/or goods used for gambling purposes.

Sports Tampering—To unlawfully alter, meddle in, or otherwise interfere with a sporting contest or event for the purpose of gaining a gambling advantage.

Homicide Offenses—The killing of one human being by another.

Murder and Nonnegligent Manslaughter—The willful (nonnegligent) killing of one human being by another.

Negligent Manslaughter—The killing of another person through negligence.

Human Trafficking Offenses—The inducement of a person to perform a commercial sex act, or labor, or services, through force, fraud, or coercion. Human trafficking has also occurred if a person under 18 years of age has been induced, or enticed, regardless of force, fraud, or coercion, to perform a commercial sex act.

Commercial Sex Acts—Inducing a person by force, fraud, or coercion to participate in commercial sex acts, or in which the person induced to perform such act(s) has not attained 18 years of age.

Involuntary Servitude—The obtaining of a person(s) through recruitment, harboring, transportation, or provision, and subjecting such persons by force, fraud, or coercion into voluntary servitude, peonage, debt bondage, or slavery (not to include commercial sex acts).

Kidnapping/Abduction—The unlawful seizure, transportation, and/or detention of a person against his/her will, or of a minor without the consent of his/her custodial parent(s) or legal guardian.

Larceny/Theft Offenses—The unlawful taking, carrying, leading, or riding away of property from the possession, or constructive possession, of another person.

Pocket-picking—The theft of articles from another person's physical possession by stealth where the victim usually does not become immediately aware of the theft.

Purse-snatching—The grabbing or snatching of a purse, handbag, etc., from the physical possession of another person.

Shoplifting—The theft, by someone other than an employee of the victim, of goods or merchandise exposed for sale.

Theft From Building—A theft from within a building which is either open to the general public or where the offender has legal access.

Theft From Coin-Operated Machine or Device—A theft from a machine or device which is operated or activated by the use of coins.

Theft From Motor Vehicle—(Except "Theft of Motor Vehicle Parts or Accessories") The theft of articles from a motor vehicle, whether locked or unlocked.

Theft of Motor Vehicle Parts or Accessories—The theft of any part or accessory affixed to the interior or exterior of a motor vehicle in a manner which would make the item an attachment of the vehicle, or necessary for its operation.

All Other Larceny—All thefts which do not fit any of the definitions of the specific subcategories of Larceny/Theft listed above.

Motor Vehicle Theft—The theft of a motor vehicle.

Pornography/Obscene Material—The violation of laws or ordinances prohibiting the manufacture, publishing, sale, purchase, or possession of sexually explicit material, e.g., literature, photographs, etc.

Prostitution Offenses—To unlawfully engage in or promote sexual activities for anything of value.

Prostitution—To engage in commercial sex acts for anything of value.

Assisting or Promoting Prostitution—To solicit customers or transport persons for prostitution purposes; to own, manage, or operate a dwelling or other establishment for the purpose of providing a place where prostitution is performed; or to otherwise assist or promote prostitution.

Purchasing Prostitution—To purchase or trade anything of value for commercial sex acts.

Robbery—The taking, or attempting to take, anything of value under confrontational circumstances from the control, custody, or care of another person by force or threat of force or violence and/or by putting the victim in fear of immediate harm.

Sex Offenses—Any sexual act directed against another person, without the consent of the victim including instances where the victim is incapable of giving consent.

Rape—(Except "Statutory Rape") The carnal knowledge of a person, without the consent of the victim, including instances where the victim is incapable of giving consent because of his/her youth or because of his/her temporary or permanent mental or physical incapacity.
Sodomy—Oral or anal sexual intercourse with another person, without the consent of the victim including instances where the victim is incapable of giving consent because of his/her youth or because of his/her temporary or permanent mental or physical incapacity.
Sexual Assault With An Object—To use an object or instrument to unlawfully penetrate, however slightly, the genital or anal opening of the body of another person, including instances where the victim is incapable of giving consent because of his/her youth or because of his/her temporary or permanent mental or physical incapacity.
Fondling—The touching of the private body parts of another person for the purpose of sexual gratification, without the consent of the victim, including instances where the victim is incapable of giving consent because of his/her youth or because of his/her temporary or permanent mental or physical incapacity.

Sex Offenses, Nonforcible—(Except "Prostitution Offenses") Unlawful, nonforcible sexual intercourse.

Incest—Nonforcible sexual intercourse between persons who are related to each other within the degrees wherein marriage is prohibited by law.
Statutory Rape—Nonforcible sexual intercourse with a person who is under the statutory age of consent.

Stolen Property Offenses—Receiving, buying, selling, possessing, concealing, or transporting any property with the knowledge that it has been unlawfully taken, as by Burglary, Embezzlement, Fraud, Larceny, Robbery, etc.

Weapon Law Violations—The violation of laws or ordinances prohibiting the manufacture, sale, purchase, transportation, possession, concealment, or use of firearms, cutting instruments, explosives, incendiary devices, or other deadly weapons.

B.2. SRS Offenses and Definitions

Murder—The willful (nonnegligent) killing of one human being by another. Deaths caused by negligence, attempts to kill, assaults to kill, suicides, accidental deaths, and justifiable homicides are excluded.

Rape—Penetration, no matter how slight, of the vagina or anus with any body part or object, or oral penetration by a sex organ of another person, without the consent of the victim. [Offenses include: Rape, Sodomy, and Sexual Assault with an Object].

Robbery—The taking or attempting to take anything of value from the care, custody, or control of a person or persons by force or threat of force or violence and/or by putting the victim in fear.

Aggravated Assault—An unlawful attack by one person upon another for the purpose of inflicting severe or aggravated bodily injury. This type of assault usually is accompanied by the use of a weapon or by means likely to produce death or great bodily harm. Simple assaults are excluded.

Burglary (Breaking or Entering)—The unlawful entry of a structure to commit a felony or a theft. Attempted forcible entry is included.

Larceny-theft (Except Motor Vehicle Theft)—The unlawful taking, carrying, leading, or riding away of property from the possession or constructive possession of another. Examples are thefts of bicycles or automobile accessories, shoplifting, pocket-picking, or the stealing of any property or article which is not taken by force and violence or by fraud. Attempted larcenies are included. Embezzlement, confidence games, forgery, worthless checks, etc., are excluded.

Motor Vehicle Theft—The theft or attempted theft of a motor vehicle. A motor vehicle is self– propelled and runs on the surface and not on rails. Specifically excluded from this category are motorboats, construction equipment, airplanes, and farming equipment.

Arson—Any willful or malicious burning or attempt to burn, with or without intent to defraud, a dwelling house, public building, motor vehicle or aircraft, personal property of another, etc.

Simple Assault—An unlawful physical attack by one person upon another where neither the offender displays a weapon, nor the victim suffers obvious severe or aggravated bodily injury involving apparent broken bones, loss of teeth, possible internal injury, severe laceration, or loss of consciousness.

Intimidation—To unlawfully place another person in reasonable fear of bodily harm through the use of threatening words and/or other conduct, but without displaying a weapon or subjecting the victim to actual physical attack.

Destruction/Damage/Vandalism of Property—To willfully or maliciously destroy, damage, deface, or otherwise injure real or personal property without the consent of the owner or the person having custody or control of it.

Human Trafficking, Commercial Sex Acts—Inducing a person by force, fraud, or coercion to participate in commercial sex acts, or in which the person induced to perform such act(s) has not attained 18 years of age.

Human Trafficking, Involuntary Servitude—The obtaining of a person(s) through recruitment, harboring, transportation, or provision, and subjecting such persons by force, fraud, or coercion into voluntary servitude, peonage, debt bondage, or slavery (not to include commercial sex acts).

B.3. Mutually Exclusive/Lesser Included Offenses

In the hate crime data collection, more than one offense can be reported within each incident once it is determined the offense(s) was motivated by bias. Certain combinations of offenses, however, cannot occur to the same victim.

Mutually Exclusive offenses cannot occur to the same victim according to UCR definitions. For example:

> Aggravated assault is a **lesser included** offense of murder, rape, sodomy, sexual assault with an object, and robbery.

Lesser Included offenses include one offense that also has an element of another offense and cannot be reported as having happened to the victim along with the other offense.

> Intimidation is a **lesser included** offense of simple assault. Therefore, one person cannot be a victim of a simple assault and an intimidation within the same incident.

Mutually Exclusive and Lesser Included Offenses are shown in the table below.

Table 5. Mutually Exclusive/Lesser Included Offenses

Offense	Offense Type	Offense(s)
Murder and Nonnegligent Manslaughter	Mutually Exclusive	Negligent Manslaughter
	Lesser Included	Aggravated Assault, Simple Assault, and Intimidation
Negligent Manslaughter	Mutually Exclusive	Murder, Aggravated Assault, Simple Assault, and Intimidation
Rape	Mutually Exclusive	Incest and Statutory Rape
	Lesser Included	Murder, Aggravated Assault, Simple Assault, Intimidation, and Fondling
Sodomy	Mutually Exclusive	Incest and Statutory Rape
	Lesser Included	Murder, Aggravated Assault, Simple Assault, Intimidation, and Fondling
Sexual Assault With An Object	Mutually Exclusive	Incest and Statutory Rape
	Lesser Included	Murder, Aggravated Assault, Simple Assault, Intimidation, and Fondling
Fondling	Mutually Exclusive	Incest and Statutory Rape
	Lesser Included	Simple Assault and Intimidation
Robbery	Lesser Included	Aggravated Assault, Simple Assault, Intimidation, Larceny-Theft Offenses, and Motor Vehicle Theft
Aggravated Assault	Lesser Included	Simple Assault and Intimidation
Simple Assault	Lesser Included	Intimidation
Incest	Mutually Exclusive	Rape, Sodomy, Sexual Assault With An Object, and Fondling
Statutory Rape	Mutually Exclusive	Rape, Sodomy, Sexual Assault With An Object, and Fondling

APPENDIX C. UCR HATE CRIME STATISTICS DATA

The FBI Uniform Crime Reporting (UCR) Program annually publishes *Hate Crime Statistics*. This publication includes data on criminal offenses that are motivated, in whole or in part, by the offender's bias against a race, religion, disability, sexual orientation, ethnicity, gender, or gender identity.

More detailed data (e.g., the subcategory breakdowns of bias motivations, the known offenders' races, and the victim types for each agency submitting hate crime data to the FBI UCR Program) are furnished in the FBI UCR Program's Hate Crime Master Files. For information on obtaining these data, please contact the FBI's Criminal Justice Information Services Division via e-mail at cjis_comm@leo.gov.

APPENDIX D. THE OFFICE OF MANAGEMENT AND BUDGET'S (OMB) RACE/ETHNICITY STANDARDS

The OMB is part of the Executive Office of the President. The OMB is comprised of four resource management offices, which were created by statute. The Paperwork Reduction Act (PRA) of 1995 (44 U.S.C. Chapter 35) established the Office of Information and Regulatory Affairs within the OMB to develop and oversee the implementation of Government-wide policies, principles, standards, and guidelines concerning statistical collection procedures and methods. The PRA covers all aspects of Federal information resources management, including OMB review and approval of agency information collection. This oversight involves a triennial review and approval of all FBI UCR Program reporting forms. Therefore, compliance with the OMB's directives is imperative to the FBI UCR Program's operations.

In 1994, in response to the need to reflect the increasing diversity of the population of the United States, OMB began a comprehensive review of the racial and ethnic categories being used in collaboration with the Interagency Committee for the Review of the Racial and Ethnic Standards. The OMB accepted the recommendations of the Interagency Committee in 1997 and released standards for federal data on race. Since the FBI UCR Program had been granted a temporary variance, the program held the changes in abeyance until its data submission methods were updated. In order to conform to the new guidelines, the FBI issued its own guidance on how law enforcement agencies should collect and maintain race and ethnicity data. These revised standards have two categories for data on ethnicity and five minimum categories for data on race. The new categories and their definitions can be found in Section 3 of this manual.

APPENDIX E. DISTINGUISHING SEXUAL ORIENTATION, GENDER IDENTITY, ANTI-TRANSGENDER, AND ANTI-GENDER NONCONFORMING CRIMES

In 2010, the FBI Uniform Crime Reporting (UCR) Program staff, through a collaborative effort with the Anti-Defamation League, began working with the national Hate Crime Coalition to establish the groundwork for the collection of data about gender and gender identity hate crimes. The national Hate Crime Coalition—made up of civil rights, religious, law enforcement, civic, and professional organizations—also formed a Gender and Gender Identity Working Group (GGIWG). The GGIWG consisted of members from the American Association of University Women (AAUW), the Human Rights Campaign, the Leadership Council on Civil and Human Rights, and the National Gay and Lesbian Task Force. The FBI UCR Program partnered with the GGIWG to draft training scenarios reflecting present-day situations encountered by victims concerning gender, sexual orientation, and gender identity. The GGIWG also requested the following information be available to further assist law enforcement with investigating potential hate crimes motivated by gender and gender identity biases, and to help determine the differences between the two categories (Gender and Gender Identity) and their subcategories (Gender–Male and Female; Gender Identity–Transgender and Gender Nonconforming).

E.1. Sexual Orientation vs. Gender Identity-Motivated Crimes

Transgender and gender nonconforming people may be of any sexual orientation (gay, lesbian, bisexual, or heterosexual). Knowing about a person's gender identity (as transgender or gender nonconforming) does not tell you anything about their sexual orientation. They are separate categories.

When crimes are committed against people based on sexual orientation or gender identity, epithets often reveal the motive for the attack. Typical gender identity-related epithets and terms include: "he-she," "she-male," "tranny," "it," and "transvestite." Also, the terms "cross dresser" and "drag queen" may be used in a hateful way, even though some individuals may self-identify with these terms. It is common for perpetrators of anti-transgender hate crimes to attack the victim after learning the victim is transgender.

Confusion in classifying the motive of a crime can occur when a perpetrator is motivated solely because of the victim's gender identity but uses an anti-gay term as well. They do this because they are often more familiar with anti-gay terms like "faggot," "dyke," and "queer," not because they are actually motivated by bias toward the victim's sexual orientation. Therefore, a perpetrator may use anti-gay epithets, even though they have targeted a person entirely because the victim is transgender or gender nonconforming.

E.2. Anti-Transgender vs. Anti-Gender Nonconforming Motivated Crimes

It may not always be obvious whether or not a crime should be classified as "anti-transgender" or "anti-gender nonconforming." Anti-transgender is the category for crimes that are committed primarily because the person lives/presents as a gender different than their sex at birth; for example, crimes that involve someone who identifies as a woman but was born male, or vice versa. Persons may identify themselves as "transgender" or "transsexual." Also, if this person is cross-dressing but has not changed to the gender they identify with, that is also an anti-transgender crime; for example, if a man wearing a dress is attacked after leaving a party that would be an anti-transgender crime. A possible indication that the crime is antitransgender is if the word(s) "transgender," "transsexual," "tranny," "transvestite," "drag king," or "drag queen," is used in the commission of a crime.

Anti-gender nonconforming crimes involve people whose appearance is only slightly gender nonconforming—they are not presenting 100 percent as the other gender. An example would be a male who wears men's clothes and identifies as a male, but wears eye-makeup; when he is attacked for that reason, this is a gender nonconforming crime. The opposite example is a woman who identifies as a woman, but wears a male item of clothing like a tie, and is attacked for that reason. A possible indication that the incident was an anti-gender nonconforming bias is if the word(s) "sissy," "lady," "girlie man," or "tomboy" is used in the commission of a crime.

E.3. Working with Transgender Victims/Witnesses

Transgender people should be addressed according to the gender they identify and live as now, regardless of the gender they were born as. If someone identifies as a woman (even if born male), she should be addressed as a woman, by using "she," "her," and "Ms." To refer to her, use her preferred name (even if she has not yet legally changed her name). If someone identifies as a man (even if born female), then he should be addressed as a man, with male pronouns, and his preferred name.

If you need to refer to someone's gender identity, the term transgender is the safest to use. In addition, it is important to know that the term transgender is an adjective, and should not be changed to "transgendered" or "transgenders." If you do not know if someone should be referred to with female or male pronouns, it is acceptable to ask that person their preferred pronoun.

E.4. Reporting Victim Sex in the NIBRS if an Anti-Transgender Bias Occurs

The NIBRS collects more detailed data on the victims, offenders, and the circumstances of crime. For example, a NIBRS participating law enforcement agency should report within an incident the age, sex, race, and ethnicity of the victim for each Crime Against Person offense. If the committed offense was bias motivated, or specifically involved an Anti-Transgender Bias, the agency should report the victim's sex as the gender identity expressed by the victim. Whereas on the Hate Crime Incident Report, if the victim type is Individual, only the total number of victims, total victims 18 years of age, and total victims under 18 years of age are collected.

Appendix F. Distinguishing between Anti-Arab, Anti-Hindu, Anti-Muslim, and Anti-Sikh Hate Crimes

In 2013, the FBI Uniform Crime Reporting (UCR) Program, the Anti-Defamation League, and the national Hate Crime Coalition began collaborating to help identify bias-motivated crimes directed toward members of the Sikh, Hindu, and Arab communities. Specifically, members of these communities from the American-Arab Anti-Discrimination Committee (ADC), the Hindu American Foundation (HAF), the Sikh Coalition, and the Sikh American Legal Defense and Education Fund (SALDEF), assisted the FBI UCR Program in developing training scenarios depicting the situations that victims of hate crimes against these groups have encountered. Coalition members further requested that the following information be available to assist law enforcement when investigating potential hate crimes motivated by biases against individuals who are of Arab ancestry, or the Hindu, Muslim, or Sikh religions, and to help distinguish the differences of each group.

F.1. Special Considerations When Working with Victims from Arab, Hindu, Muslim, Sikh, and South Asian Communities

Cultural and religious practices of Arab, Hindu, Muslim, Sikh, and South Asian community members are unique to the individual, as with any race, ethnicity, and religion. Each individual might engage in practices that are different from another individual. In light of these differences, it is important to avoid making generalizations and engage each person on an individual basis to understand their practice, while remaining sensitive and respectful. For example, as an investigator entering a house of worship or religiously sensitive area, it is always helpful to ask an appropriate person for guidance (e.g., whether to take off one's shoes)— obviously, depending on the urgency of the situation.

Additionally, these communities may face language barriers, or be hesitant to interact with police officers because of fear or previous experiences with law enforcement whether in the United States or their countries of origin. Many people in these communities come from places where, for a number of reasons, an individual might not contact the police. Building trust with members of these communities is essential, particularly in light of the post-9/11 backlash that many individuals in these communities have faced through suspicion, or ignorance.

It is important to be sensitive to these issues, to engage individuals, and to build trust with individuals and communities to create an environment that encourages individuals to report hate crimes and for witnesses to come forward and assist with investigations. Sensitive and successful outreach advances police-community relations and enhances safety nationwide.

F.2. Identifying Anti-Arab Hate Crimes

Arabs are a diverse group of people who have their origins in one of the twenty-two different countries in the Middle East and North Africa. Like biases against most ethnic groups, hate crimes against Arabs are often motivated by misunderstanding, misperceptions, stereotypes about their culture and heritage. For example, not all Arabs are Muslim, and the majority of Arabs in the United States are Christian.

When crimes are committed based on anti-Arab bias, epithets often reveal the motive for the attack. Many epithets are used to stereotype Arabs and most are intended to be an attack on their background. Typical anti-Arab epithets include: "terrorist," "camel jockey," "sand nigger," "towel head," "suicide bomber," and "America-hater." At times, a perpetrator may use the term "Ayy-rab" which is an offensive pronunciation of their ethnicity. Hate crime perpetrators sometimes use the terms "Al-Qaeda," "Hamas," "Hezbollah," "Bin Laden," or Saddam" to harass the victim based upon perceived race/ethnicity, religion, or national origin.

Often victims are attacked after the perpetrator hears a person speaking the Arabic language, sees an Arabic sign in an establishment's window, or sees the victim reading Arabic.

F.2.1. Working with Arab Victims/Witnesses

Arab victims may be hesitant to tell police officers about their Arab heritage, especially because the victim has just experienced violence or vandalism, possibly because of this heritage. As when working with any crime victim, it is important that officers communicate why they are asking questions about the victim's background. The officer should explain that questions about the victim's background are for the purpose of a crime investigation and will help determine whether or not a hate crime occurred. Arab victims and witnesses will be more likely to cooperate and answer questions if they are assured that the officer is merely trying to document the crime, determine if it was a hate crime, and prevent it from occurring in the future.

F.3. Identifying Anti-Hindu Hate Crimes

Hindu Americans targeted for hate crimes commonly face anti-Hindu epithets. Such epithets may include "dothead," "cow-kisser," or "macaca." Additionally, Hindus may also be targeted with epithets more commonly directed at Muslims or Sikhs, such as “raghead,” “towelhead,” or “terrorist.” Such epithets are sometimes sparked by Hindus wearing head coverings during religious festivals.

Hindu houses of worship are also frequent targets of hate crimes. There are many categories of Hindu houses of worship, including mandirs (temples), ashrams (hermitages), dhams (retreats), and balavihars (Sunday schools). Hindu houses of worship bear several markers, which may identify them to potential attackers. First, many mandirs are distinguished by their architecture, which includes large columns, spires, and intricate stone-carvings. Additionally, many houses of worship also maintain large bells, which are frequently rung by devotees. Furthermore, many houses of worship maintain large signs with English, Hindi, and Sanskrit lettering identifying the facility for congregants. Some Hindu temples may also display the “om” symbol or the “swastika” symbol, which is a holy symbol in the Hindu, Buddhist, and Jain faiths.

F.3.1. Hindu vs. Indian/South Asian

Although a South Asian American can be identified by ethnic origin such as India, Pakistan, Bangladesh, Sri Lanka, Nepal, or Bhutan, among others, a Hindu American is a practitioner of the Hindu faith. An individual’s identity as a Hindu American should not be confused with their identity as a South Asian American.

While the majority of Hindu Americans in the United States are of Indian origin, there are also Hindu Americans of Caucasian, African American, Hispanic, Caribbean Islander, and East Asian origin. There are approximately one million Hindu Americans who are not of South Asian origin.

F.3.2. Working with Hindu Victims/Witnesses

Some Hindus may be uncomfortable with bodily contact, and as such, may prefer to greet officers by pressing their palms together and offering a greeting of “Namaste.” It is important to avoid phrases such as “your gods.” and “idols,” as such terms may be alienating and disrespectful. Instead, terms such as “the deities” or “the murtis” are more appropriate.

F.4. Identifying Anti-Sikh Hate Crimes

Classifying a hate crime can be confusing when a perpetrator commits a bias-motivated act based upon a victim’s religious clothing, object, or identity marker, but uses epithets commonly directed at members of the Arab, Muslim, Hindu, Sikh, and South Asian communities, such as "raghead," "towelhead," and "terrorist." In such cases, officers should classify the crime based on the religion or religious practice the investigation determines was the targeted group. For example, if the investigation determines the offender's actions were motivated by and directed at a victim's dastaar (Sikh turban) and/or the kesh (unshorn hair, including a beard), the incident should be classified as Anti-Sikh. However, if the investigation shows the victim's religious article, e.g., turban, was targeted because the offender believed the victim to be a Hindu or a Muslim, the crime should be classified as Anti-Hindu or Anti-Islamic (Muslim).

APPENDIX G. DEPARTMENT OF JUSTICE, COMMUNITY RELATIONS SERVICE, REGIONAL OFFICES

The Community Relations Service (CRS) serves as *"America's Peacemaker"* for the U.S. Department of Justice. CRS helps local communities address community conflicts and tensions arising from differences of race, color, and national origin. CRS also helps communities develop strategies to prevent and respond to violent hate crimes committed on the basis of actual or perceived race, color, national origin, gender, gender identity, sexual orientation, religion and disability. CRS does not take sides in a dispute, and it does not investigate, prosecute, impose solutions, assign blame, or assess fault. By providing mediation, facilitation, training, and consulting services, CRS helps communities enhance their ability to independently prevent and resolve future conflicts.

Additionally, the CRS provides free Arab, Muslim, Sikh, Hindu, and Transgender Cultural Competency Programs. These programs are offered in 2 to 4 hour segments and Roll Call training which are intended to familiarize law enforcement and government officials with recognized customs and cultural aspects of such groups as Arab, Muslim, Sikh, Hindu, and Transgender communities. These programs were designed as an effective tool for helping law enforcement improve their understanding, partnership, outreach, and reporting mechanism with these communities. These programs can be utilized at <www.justice.gov/crs>.

Kansas City, MO 64106
(816) 426-7434

Rocky Mountain Regional Office (Serving: CO, MT, ND, SD, UT, WY)
U.S. Department of Justice
Community Relations Service
1244 Speer Boulevard, Suite 650
Denver, CO 80204-3584
(303) 844-2973

Western Regional Office (Serving: AZ, CA, HI, NV, Guam)
U.S. Department of Justice
Community Relations Service
888 South Figueroa Street, Suite 2010
Los Angeles, CA 90017
(213) 894-2941

Field Office:
U.S. Department of Justice
Community Relations Service
90 Seventh Street, Suite 3-300
San Francisco, CA 94103 (415) 744-6565

Northwest Regional Office (Serving: AK, ID, OR, WA)
U.S. Department of Justice
Community Relations Service
915 Second Avenue, Suite 1808
Seattle, WA 98174
(206) 220-6700

Appendix H. Organizations Offering Information Concerning Anti-Bias Education

American Arab Anti-Discrimination Committee
1990 M Street, NW, Suite 610
Washington, DC 20036; www.adc.org

American Association of University Women
1111 Sixteenth Street, NW
Washington, DC 20036
www.aauw.org

Anti-Defamation League
605 Third Avenue
New York, NY
10158-3560 www.adl.org

Hindu American Foundation
910 Seventeenth St. NW, Suite 316A
Washington, DC 20006
www.hafsite.org

Human Rights Campaign
1640 Rhode Island Avenue, NW
Washington, DC 20036
www.hrc.org

International Association of Chiefs of Police
44 Canal Center Plaza, Suite 200
Alexandria, VA 22314
http://www.theiacp.org

The Leadership Conference on Civil and Human Rights
1629 K Street, NW
10th Floor
Washington, DC 20006
www.civilrights.org

National Center for Transgender Equality
1325 Massachusetts Avenue, NW
Washington, DC 20005 http://transequality.org

National Council of Jewish Women (NCJW)
241 West 72nd Street
New York, NY 10023
http://www.ncjw.org

National Disability Rights Network
900 Second Street, NE, Suite
211 Washington, DC 20002
http://www.napas.org

National Gay and Lesbian Task Force
1325 Massachusetts Avenue, NW, Suite 600
Washington, DC 20005
www.theTaskForce.org

Sikh American Legal Defense and Education Fund
1012 14th Street, NW, Suite 450
Washington, DC 20005
www.saldef.org

The Sikh Coalition
PO Box 11258
Washington, DC 20008 www.sikhcoalition.org

In: Hate Crime Data Collection
Editors: Gloria Thompson
ISBN: 978-1-63483-624-1

Chapter 2

HATE CRIME VICTIMIZATION, 2004–2012 - STATISTICAL TABLES*

Meagan Meuchel Wilson

In 2012, an estimated 293,800 nonfatal violent and property hate crime victimizations occurred against persons age 12 or older residing in U.S. households. The apparent increase from 2011 to 2012 in the rate of overall violent hate crime was not statistically significant (Figure 1).

The findings from this report came primarily from the Bureau of Justice Statistics' (BJS) National Crime Victimization Survey (NCVS), which has been collecting data on crimes motivated by hate since 2003. The NCVS and the FBI's Uniform Crime Reports (UCR) Hate Crime Statistics Program, which are the principal sources of annual information on hate crime in the United States, use the definition of hate crime provided in the Hate Crime Statistics Act (28 U.S.C. § 534). The act defines hate crimes as "crimes that manifest evidence of prejudice based on race, gender or gender identity, religion, disability, sexual orientation, or ethnicity." The NCVS measures crimes perceived by victims to be motivated by an offender's bias against them for belonging to or being associated with a group largely identified by these characteristics.

Hate crime victimization refers to a single victim or household that experienced a criminal incident believed by the victim to be motivated by hate. For violent crimes (rape or sexual assault, robbery, aggravated assault, and

* This is an edited, reformatted and augmented version of Bureau of Justice Statistics report, NCJ 244409, issued February 2014.

simple assault) and for personal larceny, the count of hate crime victimizations is the number of individuals who experienced a violent hate crime. For crimes against households (burglary, motor vehicle theft, and other theft), each household affected by a hate crime is counted as a single victimization.

This report presents NCVS data on the characteristics of hate crimes and hate crime victims from 2003 to 2012. Trend estimates are based on 2-year rolling averages centered on the most recent year. This method generally improves the reliability and stability of estimate comparisons over time. For ease of discussion, the report refers to all 2-year estimates by the most recent year. For example, estimates reported for 2012 represent the average estimates for 2011 and 2012. The report also compares NCVS and UCR overall trends in hate crime victimization.

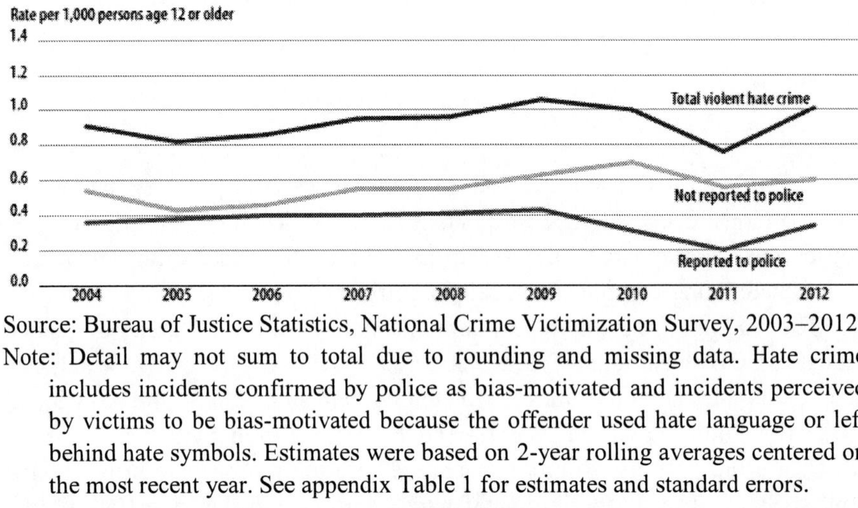

Source: Bureau of Justice Statistics, National Crime Victimization Survey, 2003–2012.
Note: Detail may not sum to total due to rounding and missing data. Hate crime includes incidents confirmed by police as bias-motivated and incidents perceived by victims to be bias-motivated because the offender used hate language or left behind hate symbols. Estimates were based on 2-year rolling averages centered on the most recent year. See appendix Table 1 for estimates and standard errors.

Figure 1. Violent hate crime victimizations reported and not reported to police, 2004–2012

Number and Rate of Hate Crimes

- In 2012, hate crimes accounted for 1.2% of all victimizations and 4.2% of violent victimizations (Table 1).
- No statistically significant change was observed in either the number of total hate crimes or violent hate crimes that occurred from 2004 to 2012.

- After a decline from 2004 to 2005, the property hate crime victimization rate remained stable from 2005 to 2012.

Hate Crime Motivation

- Approximately 58% of hate crime victims reported more than one type of motivation in 2012 (not shown in Table).
- In 2012, victims perceived that the offender was motivated by bias against the victim's ethnicity in 51% of hate crimes (Table 2). This was a statistically significant increase from 30% of hate crimes motivated by ethnicity bias in 2011 and 22% in 2004.
- The percentage of hate crimes motivated by religious bias was nearly three times higher in 2012 (28%) than in 2004 (10%), but did not have a statistically significant change from 2011 to 2012.
- In 2009, Congress passed new legislation amending the Hate Crime Statistics Act to include hate crimes with evidence of bias against a particular gender or gender identity. BJS has been collecting information on hate crimes motivated by gender bias since 2003. The percentage of hate crimes motivated by gender bias was more than two times higher in 2011 (25%) and 2012 (26%) than in 2004 (12%).

Table 1. Hate crime victimizations, 2004–2012

	Total hate crimes[a]		Violent hate crimes[b]			Property hate crimes[c]		
Year	Number	Percent of total victimi-zations[d]	Number	Rate[e]	Percent of total violent victimi-zations[d]	Number	Rate[f]	Percent of total property victimi-zations[d]
2004	281,670	1.0%	220,060	0.9	3.1%	61,610	0.5	0.3%
2005	223,060	0.9	198,400	0.8	2.9	21,740	0.2	0.1
2006	230,490	0.8	211,730	0.9	2.8	15,830	0.1	0.1
2007	263,440	1.0	236,860	1.0	3.1	24,640	0.2	0.1
2008	266,640	1.1	241,800	1.0	3.7	22,890	0.2	0.1
2009	284,620	1.2	267,170	1.1	4.4	17,450!	0.1	0.1
2010	273,100	1.3	255,810	1.0	4.8	17,290!	0.1	0.1
2011[g]	218,010	1.0	195,880	0.8	3.6	22,130	0.2	0.1
2012	293,790	1.2	263,540	1.0	4.2	30,250	0.2	0.2

Source: Bureau of Justice Statistics, National Crime Victimization Survey, 2003–2012.

Note: Hate crime includes incidents confirmed by police as bias-motivated and incidents perceived by victims to be bias-motivated because the offender used hate language or left behind hate symbols. Estimates were based on 2-year rolling averages centered on the most recent year. Numbers rounded to the nearest ten. See appendix Table 2 for population data and appendix Table 3 for standard errors.

! Interpret with caution; estimate based on 10 or fewer cases, or the coeffcient of variation is greater than 50%.

[a] Includes violent crimes, personal larceny, and household property crimes.

[b] Includes rape or sexual assault, robbery, aggravated assault, and simple assault.

[c] Includes household burglary, motor vehicle theft, and other theft.

[d] See appendix Table 2 for number of total victimizations.

[e] Per 1,000 persons age 12 or older.

[f] Per 1,000 households.

[g] Due to a revision in the public use file, 2011 victimization counts vary slightly from previous publications.

Table 2. Victims' perceptions of offender bias in hate crimes, 2004, 2011 and 2012

Offender bias	2004	2011	2012
Ethnicity[a]	22%	30%	51%
Race	58	58	46
Association[b]	23	40	34
Religion	10	25	28
Gender	12	25	26
Sexual orientation	22	19!	13
Disability	11	22	11
Perceived characteristics[c]	19	15!	7!

Source: Bureau of Justice Statistics, National Crime Victimization Survey, 2003–2012.

Note: Hate crime includes incidents confirmed by police as bias-motivated and incidents perceived by victims to be bias-motivated because the offender used hate language or left behind hate symbols. Estimates were based on 2- year rolling averages centered on the most recent year. Detail does not sum to total due to victims reporting more than one type of bias motivating the hate-related victimizations. See appendix Table 4 for standard errors.

! Interpret with caution; estimate based on 10 or fewer cases, or the coefficient of variation is greater than 50%.

[a] Motivated by victim's ancestral, cultural, social, or national affiliation.

[b] Motivated by victim's association with people having certain characteristics.

[C] Motivated by offender's perception of victim's characteristics.

Differences Between Hate and Nonhate Crimes

- Each year from 2004 to 2012, violent crimes accounted for a higher percentage of hate crimes than nonhate crimes (Table 3).
- The percentage of hate crimes involving violence increased from 78% in 2004 to 90% in both 2011 and 2012. However, no statistically significant difference was observed in the percentage of hate crimes involving serious violence or simple assault in these years.
- In 2012, serious violent crime accounted for a higher percentage of all hate crime victimizations (27%) than nonhate crime victimizations (8%).
- In 2012, no statistically significant difference was observed between the percentage of violent hate crimes (30%) and violent nonhate crimes (31%) that involved serious violence (not shown in Table).

Weapons and Injuries

- In 2012, the offender had a weapon in at least 24% of violent hate crime victimizations (Table 4).
- No statistically significant difference was reported between the percentage of violent hate (24%) and violent nonhate (20%) crime victimizations in which the offender was known to have a weapon in 2012.
- The percentage of violent hate and violent nonhate crime victimizations in which the offender was known to have a weapon remained stable from 2011 to 2012.
- In 2012, the victim sustained an injury in about 20% of violent hate crime victimizations.
- No statistically significant difference was observed in 2012 between the percentage of violent hate (20%) and violent nonhate (24%) crime victimizations in which the victim sustained an injury.
- The percentage of violent hate and violent nonhate crime victimizations in which the victim sustained an injury remained stable from 2011 to 2012.

Table 3. Hate and nonhate crime victimizations, by type of crime, 2004, 2011, and 2012

	2004		2011		2012	
Type of crime	Hate	Nonhate	Hate	Nonhate	Hate	Nonhate
Violent[a]	78%	26%	90%	24%	90%	25%
Serious violent crime[b]	21	9	29	8	27	8
Simple assault	57	18	61	16	63	17
Property[c]	22%	73%	10%	75%	10%	75%

Source: Bureau of Justice Statistics, National Crime Victimization Survey, 2003–2012.

Note: Detail may not sum to total due to rounding. Hate crime includes incidents confirmed by police as bias-motivated and incidents perceived by victims to be bias-motivated because the offender used hate language or left behind hate symbols. Estimates were based on 2-year rolling averages centered on the most recent year.

See appendix Table 5 for standard errors.

[a] Includes rape or sexual assault, robbery, aggravated assault, and simple assault.

[b] Includes rape or sexual assault, robbery, and aggravated assault.

[c] Includes burglary, motor vehicle theft, and other theft.

Table 4. Presence of weapons and injuries sustained in violent hate

	Presence of weapon		*Any injury sustained*[c]	
Year	*Hate*[a]	*Nonhate*[b]	*Hate*	*Nonhate*[d]
2004	23%	23%	19%	28%
2005	16 !	24	17	27
2006	18	24	31	28
2007	21	23	26	28
2008	20	20	18	24
2009	28	19	16	25
2010	30	21	12	27
2011	25	21	21	26
2012	24	20	20	24

Source: Bureau of Justice Statistics, National Crime Victimization Survey, 2003–2012.

Note: Hate crime includes incidents confirmed by police as bias-motivated and incidents perceived by victims to be bias-motivated because the offender used hate language or left behind hate symbols. Estimates were based on 2-year rolling averages centered on the most recent year. See appendix Table 6 for standard errors.

! Interpret with caution; estimate based on 10 or fewer cases, or the coefficient of variation is greater than 50%.

[a] Percentage of violent hate crime victims who did not know whether the offender had a weapon (5–15%) is not shown in Table.

[b] Percentage of violent nonhate crime victims who did not know whether the offender had a weapon (6–8%) is not shown in Table.

[c] Includes minor injuries, rape injuries, and serious injuries (i.e., broken bones, lost teeth, internal injuries, loss of consciousness, and any unspecified injury requiring two or more days of hospitalization).

[d] Percentage of violent nonhate crime victims for whom it was unknown whether an injury was sustained (0.4% or less) is not shown in Table.

Hate Crimes Reported to the Police

- An estimated 60% of total and violent hate crime victimizations were not reported to police in 2012 (Table 5). This was a slight* decline from 2011, when about three-quarters of total (74%) and violent (73%) hate crime victimizations were not reported to police.
- Overall, the percentage of hate crime victimizations that resulted in the victim signing a complaint or the police making an arrest did not have a statistically significant change from 2011 to 2012.

*Differences described as slight or slightly passed a test at the 0.10 level of statistical significance (90% confidence level). Caution is required when comparing estimates not explicitly discussed in this report.

Table 5. Hate crime victimizations reported to police, 2004, 2011, and 2012

	Total				Violent	
	2004	2011	2012	2004	2011	2012
Reporteda	45%	25%	34%	39%	26%	34%
By victim	26	16	22	15	16	21
By someone else[b]	20	9	12	25	10	12
Not reported	53%	74%	60%	59%	73%	59%
Complaint signedc	13%	11%	13%	16%	12%	14%
Arrest madec	9%	6%	4%!	11%	6%!	4%!

Source: Bureau of Justice Statistics, National Crime Victimization Survey, 2003–2012.

Note: Detail may not sum to total due to rounding. Hate crime includes incidents confirmed by police as bias-motivated and incidents perceived by victims to be bias-motivated because the offender used hate language or left behind hate symbols. Hate crimes include violent crimes, personal larceny, and household property crimes. Estimates were based on 2-year rolling averages centered on the most recent year. See appendix Table 7 for standard errors.

! Interpret with caution; estimate based on 10 or fewer cases, or the coefficient of variation is greater than 50%.

[a] Percentage of victims for whom it was unknown whether the police were notified (7% or less) is not shown in Table.

[b] Includes other household members; other officials, such as guards, apartment managers, and school officials; and others.

[c] Percentages based on all hate crime victimizations, including those in which the police were not notified or it was unknown whether the police were notified.

Violent Hate Crime Victim and Offender Characteristics

- From 2011 to 2012, rates of violent hate crime victimization did not have a statistically significant change for either males or females (Table 6).
- In 2011, violent hate crime victimization rates were similar among white non-Hispanics, black non-Hispanics, and Hispanics. However, in 2012, Hispanics experienced a higher rate of violent hate crime victimization (2.0 victimizations per 1,000 residents) than whites (0.8 per 1,000) and a slightly higher rate than blacks (1.1 per 1,000).
- The rate of violent hate crime victimization against Hispanics more than tripled from 0.6 per 1,000 persons age 12 or older in 2011 to 2.0 per 1,000 in 2012.
- The rate of violent hate crime victimization increased for persons ages 18 to 24 (from 0.6 per 1,000 in 2011 to 2.0 in 2012) and for persons ages 50 to 64 (from 0.4 to 0.9 per 1,000), while the rate declined for persons ages 25 to 34 (from 1.6 to 0.7 per 1,000). Violent hate crime victimization rates for persons in all other age groups did not have a statistically significant change from 2011 to 2012.
- Persons residing in households with an income greater than $50,000 per year experienced a higher rate of violent hate crime victimization in 2012 (1.0 per 1,000) than in 2011 (0.4 per 1,000).
- In both 2011 and 2012, persons living in households with an income of $24,999 or less per year experienced the highest rate of violent hate crime victimization (2.1 per 1,000), compared to persons residing in all other households (1.0 or less per 1,0001).

Table 6. Characteristics of violent hate crime victims, 2004, 2011, and 2012

Percent					*Ratea*	
Victim characteristic	*2004*	*2011*	*2012*	*2004*	*2011*	*2012*
Sex	100%	100%	100%			
Male	60	56	53	1.1	0.9	1.1
Female	40	44	47	0.7	0.7	0.9
Race/Hispanic origin	100%	100%	100%			
White[b]	74	64	52	1.0	0.7	0.8
Black/African American[b]	4!	13!	13	0.3!	0.9!	1.1
Hispanic/Latino	17	12	30	1.2	0.6	2.0
Other[b,c]	5!	10!	5!	0.9!	1.2!	0.8!
Age	100%	100%	100%			
12–17	33	25	24	2.9	2.0	2.5
18–24	20	10	23	1.6	0.6	2.0
25–34	14	35	11	0.8	1.6	0.7
35–49	23	18	20	0.8	0.6	0.9
50–64	8	11	21	0.4	0.4	0.9
65 or older	1 !	1!	1 !	0.1!	0.1!	0.1!
Household income	100%	100%	100%			
$24,999orless	33	38	32	1.5	1.9	2.1
$25,000–$49,999	23	15	15	0.9	0.6	0.8
$50,000 or more	26	18	37	0.7	0.4	1.0
Not reported	17	28	16	0.7	0.7	0.6

Source: Bureau of Justice Statistics, National Crime Victimization Survey, 2003–2012.

Note: Detail may not sum to total due to rounding. Hate crime includes incidents confirmed by police as bias-motivated and incidents perceived by victims to be bias-motivated because the offender used hate language or left behind hate symbols. Violent hate crimes include rape or sexual assault, robbery, aggravated assault, and simple assault. Estimates were based on 2-year rolling averages centered on the most recent year. See appendix Table 8 for standard errors.

! Interpret with caution; estimate based on 10 or fewer cases, or the coefficient of variation is greater than 50%.

[a] Per 1,000 persons age 12 or older in each category.

[b] Excludes persons of Hispanic or Latino origin.

[c] Includes persons identified as American Indian or Alaska Native; Asian, Native Hawaiian, or other Pacific Islander; and two or more races.

- From 2011 to 2012, no statistically significant change was observed in the percentage of violent hate crimes committed by either a single offender or by multiple offenders (Table 7).

- In 2012, the percentage of violent hate crimes committed by a single offender (64%) was higher than the percentage committed by two or more offenders (34%).
- Each year from 2004 to 2012, victims reported that males committed the majority of violent hate crimes.
- The percentage of violent hate crime victims who perceived the offender to be white decreased from 58% in 2011 to 34% in 2012. However, the percentage of white offenders was similar in 2004 and 2012.
- The percentage of offenders ages 18 to 29 declined from 29% in 2011 to 13% in 2012. In 2012, persons age 30 and over made up the largest percentage of hate crime offenders (41%).
- In 2012, the percentage of violent hate crimes committed by someone known to the victim was slightly higher (53%) than the percentage committed by a stranger (40%).

Hate Crimes Recorded by the NCVS and UCR

- The FBI's UCR collects data on hate crimes known to the police. It includes offenses excluded from the NCVS, such as murder or nonnegligent manslaughter, intimidation, arson, vandalism, and crimes against institutions (e.g., churches, synagogues, and businesses). The NCVS collects data on hate crimes both reported and not reported to police and allows the victim to define whether a hate crime occurred.
- Hate crime victimizations recorded by the UCR declined steadily from 2008 to 2012 (Table 8). However, no statistically significant change was observed in NCVS hate crime victimizations reported to police from 2008 to 2012.
- UCR hate crime victimizations were lower in 2012 than in 2004. No statistically significant difference was observed between the number of NCVS hate crime victimizations reported to police in 2004 (127,390) and 2012 (98,460).

Table 7. Characteristics of violent hate crime offenders as reported by victims, 2004, 2011, and 2012

Offender characteristic	2004	2011	2012
Number of offenders	100%	100%	100%
One	71	57	64
Twoormore	27	42	34
Unknown	2!	1!	2!
Sex	100%	100%	100%
Male	66	65	61
Female	27	24	16
Bothmale and female	3!	10!	8!
Unknown	3!	2!	15!
Race	100%	100%	100%
White	30	58	34
Black/African American	41	24	32
Other[a]	17	5!	17!
Variousraces[b]	7!	7!	6!
Unknown	6!	6!	11!
Age	100%	100%	100%
17or younger	28	23	19
18–29	20	29	13
30 or older	24	34	41
Two or moreagegroups	22	8!	10
Unknown	6!	6!	17!
Relationship to victim	100%	100%	100%
Intimate/family/casual acquaintance	51	61	53
Stranger	39	33	40
Unknown	11!	6!	7!

Note: Detail may not sum to total due to rounding. Hate crime includes incidents confirmed by police as bias-motivated and incidents perceived by victims to be bias-motivated because the offender used hate language or left behind hate symbols. Violent hate crimes include rape or sexual assault, robbery, aggravated assault, and simple assault. Estimates were based on 2-year rolling averages centered on the most recent year. See appendix Table 9 for standard errors.! Interpret with caution; estimate based on 10 or fewer cases, or the coefficient of variation is greater than 50%.

aIncludes persons identified as American Indian or Alaska Native; Asian, Native Hawaiian, or other Pacific Islander; and two or more races. bIncludes multiple offenders of two or more racial groups.

Source: Bureau of Justice Statistics, National Crime Victimization Survey, 2003–2012.

Table 8. Hate crime victimizations recorded by the NCVS and UCR, 2004–2012

		NCVS[a]	
Year	Not reported to police	Reported to police	UCR[b]
2004	148,020	127,390	9,310
2005	116,500	101,940	9,170
2006	122,120	108,370	9,230
2007	152,680	110,760	9,590
2008	155,090	111,550	9,610
2009	171,150	113,470	9,010
2010	189,390	83,710	8,270
2011	161,970	53,970	7,960
2012	177,130	98,460	7,440

Note: Hate crime includes incidents confirmed by police as bias-motivated and incidents perceived by victims to be bias-motivated because the offender used hate language or left behind hate symbols. Estimates were based on 2-year rolling averages centered on the most recent year. Numbers rounded to the nearest ten. See appendix Table 10 for standard errors.

[a] The number of hate crime victimizations for which it was unknown whether the police were notified (6% or less) is not shown in Table.

[b] Includes murder/nonnegligent manslaughter, forcible rape, aggravated assault, simple assault, intimidation, other crimes against persons, robbery, burglary, larceny-theft, motor vehicle theft, arson, destruction/vandalism, other crimes against property, and crimes against society. Excludes crimes against juveniles. Source: Bureau of Justice Statistics, based on files provided by the FBI, Uniform Crime Reporting Program, Hate Crime Statistics, 2003–2012; and National Crime Victimization Survey, 2003–2012.

Based on data from the NCVS, persons age 12 or older experienced an annual average of 269,140 hate crime victimizations from 2004 to 2012, of which 105,890 were reported to police (Figure 2).

According to the NCVS, an annual average of 14,380 hate crime victimizations were confirmed by police investigators from 2004 to 2012. This estimate was not statistically different from the FBI's UCR annual average number of hate crime victims (8,770) during the same period.

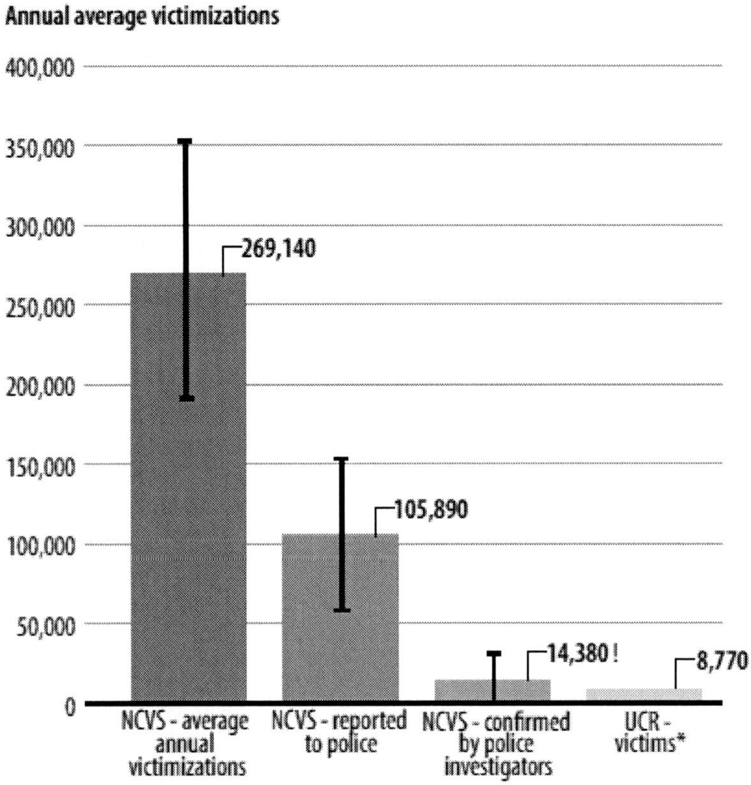

Source: Bureau of Justice Statistics, based on files provided by the FBI, Uniform Crime Reporting Program, Hate Crime Statistics, 2003–2012; and National Crime Victimization Survey, 2003–2012.

Note: Hate crime includes incidents confirmed by police as bias-motivated and incidents perceived by victims to be bias-motivated because the offender used hate language or left behind hate symbols. Estimates were based on 10-year rolling averages due to small sample sizes. Numbers rounded to the nearest ten.

Error bars on NCVS estimates are based on 95% confidence levels. The standard error for average annual victimizations is 40,701; reported to police is 24,180; and confirmed by police investigators is 8,345.

*Includes murder/nonnegligent manslaughter, forcible rape, aggravated assault, simple assault, intimidation, other crimes against persons, robbery, burglary, larceny-theft, motor vehicle theft, arson, destruction/vandalism, other crimes against property, and crimes against society.

! Interpret with caution; estimate based on 10 or fewer cases, or the coeffcient of variation is greater than 50%.

Figure 2. NCVS and UCR hate crime victimizations, 2004–2012.

METHODOLOGY

Survey Coverage

The National Crime Victimization Survey (NCVS) is an annual data collection conducted by the U.S. Census Bureau for the Bureau of Justice Statistics (BJS). The NCVS is a self-report survey in which interviewed persons are asked about the number and characteristics of victimizations experienced during the prior 6 months. The NCVS collects information on nonfatal personal crimes (rape or sexual assault, robbery, aggravated and simple assault, and personal larceny) and household property crimes (burglary, motor vehicle theft, and other theft) both reported and not reported to police. In addition to providing annual level and change estimates on criminal victimization, the NCVS is the primary source of information on the nature of criminal victimization incidents.

Survey respondents provide information about themselves (e.g., age, sex, race and Hispanic origin, marital status, education level, and income) and whether they experienced a victimization. Information is collected for each victimization incident about the offender (e.g., age, race and Hispanic origin, sex, and victim-offender relationship), characteristics of the crime (including time and place of occurrence, use of weapons, nature of injury, and economic consequences), whether the crime was reported to police, reasons the crime was or was not reported, and experiences with the criminal justice system.

The NCVS is administered to persons age 12 or older from a nationally representative sample of households in the United States. The NCVS defines a household as a group of members who all reside at a sampled address. Persons are considered household members when the sampled address is their usual place of residence at the time of the interview and when they have no usual place of residence elsewhere. Once selected, households remain in the sample for 3 years, and eligible persons in these households are interviewed every 6 months either in-person or over the phone, for a total of seven interviews.

Generally, all first interviews are conducted in-person. New households rotate into the sample on an ongoing basis to replace outgoing households that have been in the sample for the 3-year period. The sample includes persons living in group quarters, such as dormitories, rooming houses, and religious group dwellings, and excludes persons living in military barracks and institutional settings, such as correctional or hospital facilities, and the homeless. (For more information, see the *Survey Methodology* for *Criminal Victimization in the United States, 2008*, NCJ 231173, BJS web, May 2011.)

Nonresponse and Weighting Adjustments

In 2012, 92,390 households and 162,940 persons age 12 or older were interviewed for the NCVS. Each household was interviewed twice during the year. The response rate was 87% for households and 87% for eligible persons. Victimizations that occurred outside of the United States were excluded from this report. In 2012, less than 1% of the unweighted victimizations occurred outside of the United States and were excluded from the analyses.

Estimates in this report use data from the 2003 to 2012 NCVS data files, weighted to produce annual estimates of victimization for persons age 12 or older living in U.S. households. Because the NCVS relies on a sample rather than a census of the entire U.S. population, weights are designed to inflate sample point estimates to known population totals and to compensate for survey nonresponse and other aspects of the sample design.

The NCVS data files include both household and person weights. The household weight is commonly used to calculate estimates of property crimes, such as motor vehicle theft or burglary, which are identified within the household. Person weights provide an estimate of the population represented by each person in the sample. After proper adjustment, both household and person weights are also typically used to form the denominator in calculations of crime rates.

The victimization weights used in this analysis account for the number of persons present during an incident and for high-frequency repeat victimizations (or series victimizations). Series victimizations are similar in type but occur with such frequency that a victim is unable to recall each individual event or describe each event in detail. Survey procedures allow NCVS interviewers to identify and classify these similar victimizations as series victimizations and to collect detailed information on only the most recent incident in the series.

The weight counts series incidents as the actual number of incidents reported by the victim, up to a maximum of ten incidents. Including series victimizations in national rates results in rather large increases in the level of violent victimization. However, trends in violence are generally similar regardless of whether series victimizations are included.

In 2012, series incidents accounted for about 1% of all victimizations and 4% of all violent victimizations. Weighting series incidents as the number of incidents up to a maximum often produces more reliable estimates of crime levels, while the cap at ten minimizes the effect of extreme outliers on the rates. Additional information on the series enumeration is detailed in the report

Methods for Counting High Frequency Repeat Victimizations in the National Crime Victimization Survey, NCJ 237308, BJS web, April 2012.

Due to slight revisions in the public use file weights, 2011 victimization estimates may vary slightly from previous publications. These differences were determined to be statistically insignificant changes.

Standard Error Computations

When national estimates are derived from a sample, as with the NCVS, caution must be taken when comparing one estimate to another estimate or when comparing estimates over time. Although one estimate may be larger than another, estimates based on a sample have some degree of sampling error. The sampling error of an estimate depends on several factors, including the amount of variation in the responses and the size of the sample. When the sampling error around an estimate is taken into account, the estimates that appear different may not be statistically different.

One measure of the sampling error associated with an estimate is the standard error. The standard error can vary from one estimate to the next. In general, for a given metric, an estimate with a smaller standard error provides a more reliable approximation of the true value than an estimate with a larger standard error. Estimates with relatively large standard errors are associated with less precision and reliability and should be interpreted with caution.

In order to generate standard errors around numbers and estimates from the NCVS, the Census Bureau produced generalized variance function (GVF) parameters for BJS. The GVFs take into account aspects of the NCVS complex sample design and represent the curve fitted to a selection of individual standard errors based on the Jackknife Repeated Replication technique. The GVF parameters were used to generate standard errors for each point estimate (e.g., counts, percentages, and rates) in this report.

In this report, BJS conducted tests to determine whether differences in estimated numbers and percentages were statistically significant once sampling error was taken into account. Using statistical programs developed specifically for the NCVS, BJS tested the significance of all comparisons in the text. The Student's t-statistic was the primary test procedure, which tests the difference between two sample estimates. To ensure that the observed differences between estimates were larger than might be expected due to sampling variation, the significance level was set at the 95% confidence level. Differences described as slight or slightly passed a test at the 0.10 level of statistical significance (90%

confidence level). Caution is required when comparing estimates not explicitly discussed in this report.

Data users can use the estimates and the standard errors of the estimates provided in this report to generate a confidence interval around the estimate as a measure of the margin of error. The following example illustrates how standard errors can be used to generate confidence intervals:

According to the NCVS, in 2012, the violent hate crime victimization rate among persons age 12 or older was 1.0 per 1,000 persons (see Table 1). Using the GVFs, BJS determined that the estimate has a standard error of 0.1 (see appendix Table 3). A confidence interval around the estimate was generated by multiplying the standard errors by ±1.96 (the t-score of a normal, two-tailed distribution that excludes 2.5% at either end of the distribution). Therefore, the 95% confidence interval around the 1.0 estimate from 2012 is 1.0 ± (0.1 X 1.96) or (0.8 to 1.2). In other words, if different samples using the same procedures were taken from the U.S. population in 2012, 95% of the time the violent hate crime victimization rate would fall between 0.8 and 1.2 per 1,000 persons.

In this report, a coefficient of variation (CV) for all estimates, representing the ratio of the standard error to the estimate, was also calculated for all estimates. CVs provide a measure of reliability and a means to compare the precision of estimates across measures with differing levels or metrics. In cases where the CV was greater than 50%, or the unweighted sample had 10 or fewer cases, the estimate was noted with a "!" symbol (Interpret data with caution; estimate based on 10 or fewer sample cases, or the coefficient of variation is greater than 50%).

Uniform Crime Reports (UCR)

The UCR Hate Crime Statistics Program captures information about the types of bias that motivate hate crimes, the nature of the offenses, and some information about the victims and offenders by attaching the collection of hate crime statistics to the established UCR data collection procedures. The hate crime data presented here comprise a subset of information that law enforcement agencies submit to the UCR program.

Crimes reported to the FBI involve those motivated by biases based on race, religion, sexual orientation, ethnicity/ national origin, and disability. Forthcoming data collection changes will allow the reporting of crimes motivated by gender and gender identity bias, as well as crimes committed by and directed against juveniles. The victim of a hate crime may be an individual, business, institution, or society as a whole. In UCR data, law enforcement specifies the number of offenders and, when possible, the race of the offender or offenders as a group. Agencies that participated in the Hate Crime Statistics Program in 2012 represented nearly 249 million residents, or 79.3% percent of the nation's population, covering 48 states and the District of Columbia.

Hate Crime Legislation

On April 23, 1990, Congress passed the Hate Crime Statistics Act, which requires the Attorney General to collect data "about crimes that manifest evidence of prejudice based on race, religion, sexual orientation, or ethnicity." The Attorney General delegated the responsibilities of developing the procedures for implementing, collecting, and managing hate crime data to the director of the FBI, who in turn assigned the tasks to the UCR program. Under the direction of the Attorney General and with the cooperation and assistance of many local and state law enforcement agencies, the UCR program created a hate crime data collection to comply with the congressional mandate.

In September 1994, lawmakers amended the Hate Crime Statistics Act to include bias against persons with disabilities in the Violent Crime Control and Law Enforcement Act of 1994. The FBI started gathering data for the additional bias type on January 1, 1997.

The Church Arson Prevention Act, which was signed into law in July 1996, removed the sunset clause from the original statute and mandated that the collection of hate crime data become a permanent part of the UCR program.

In 2009, Congress further amended the Hate Crime Statistics Act by passing the Matthew Shepard and James Byrd, Jr. Hate Crime Prevention Act. The amendment includes the collection of data for crimes motivated by bias against a particular gender and gender identity, as well as for crimes committed by, and crimes directed against, juveniles. The FBI is currently making plans to implement changes to collect these data.

The Hate Crime Statistics Act can be accessed at http://www2.fbi.gov/ucr/hc2009/hatecrimestatistics.html.

Appendix Table 1. Estimates and standard errors for Figure 1: Violent hate crime victimizations reported and not reported to police, 2004–2012

	Rate of violent hate crime*				Standard error	
Year	Total	Not reported to police	Reported to police	Total	Not reportedto police	Reported to police
2004	0.9	0.5	0.4	0.1	0.1	0.1
2005	0.8	0.4	0.4	0.1	0.1	0.1
2006	0.9	0.5	0.4	0.1	0.1	0.1
2007	1.0	0.5	0.4	0.1	0.1	0.1
2008	1.0	0.5	0.4	0.1	0.1	0.1
2009	1.1	0.6	0.4	0.2	0.1	0.1
2010	1.0	0.7	0.3	0.2	0.1	0.1
2011	0.8	0.6	0.2	0.1	0.1	0.1
2012	1.0	0.6	0.3	0.1	0.1	0.1

Source: Bureau of Justice Statistics, National Crime Victimization Survey, 2003–2012.

Note: Detail may not sum to total due to rounding and missing data. *Per 1,000 persons age 12 or older.

Appendix Table 2. Population and total criminal victimization counts, 2004–2012

	U.S. resident population				
	Persons age 12		Total criminal victimizations		
Year	or older	Households	All[a]	Violent[b]	Property[c]
2004	240,504,850	114,956,250	27,012,660	7,202,560	19,593,620
2005	243,104,500	116,437,690	26,097,760	6,836,930	19,034,070
2006	245,869,190	117,479,100	27,184,240	7,689,110	19,293,790
2007	248,788,980	118,680,960	27,037,130	7,622,310	19,215,320
2008	251,293,700	120,322,300	24,699,350	6,603,830	17,897,050
2009	253,174,070	121,734,360	22,933,870	6,031,350	16,750,320
2010	255,033,770	122,606,410	21,255,680	5,302,610	15,817,290
2011[d]	256,752,090	122,961,860	21,763,690	5,374,250	16,237,380
2012	259,769,280	124,479,520	24,830,300	6,327,560	18,343,060

Source: Bureau of Justice Statistics, National Crime Victimization Survey, 2003–2012.

Note: Estimates were based on 2-year rolling averages centered on the most recent year. Numbers rounded to the nearest ten.

[a] Includes violent crimes, personal larceny, and household property crimes.

[b] Includes rape or sexual assault, robbery, aggravated assault, and simple assault.

[c] Includes burglary, motor vehicle theft, and other theft.

[d] Due to a revision in the public use file, 2011 victimization counts vary slightly from previous publications.

Appendix Table 3. Standard errors for Table 1: Hate crime victimizations, 2004–2012

	Total hate crimes		Violenthatecrimes			Propertyhatecrimes		
Year	Number	Percent of total victimi-zations	Num-ber	Rate	Percent of total violent victimizations	Num-ber	Rate	Percent of total property victimizations
2004	38,150	0.1%	33,292	0.1	0.3%	16,218	0.1	0.1%
2005	36,153	0.1	33,915	0.1	0.4	9,299	0.1	--
2006	36,840	0.1	35,175	0.1	0.3	7,375	--	--
2007	39,039	0.1	36,798	0.1	0.3	10,435	0.1	--
2008	45,320	0.1	42,750	0.1	0.5	10,321	0.1	--
2009	61,025	0.2	58,627	0.2	0.7	8,907!	0.1	--
2010	54,876	0.2	52,530	0.2	0.7	9,133!	0.1	--
2011	42,840	0.2	39,880	0.1	0.6	10,119	0.1	--
2012	48,156	0.1	44,941	0.1	0.5	12,029	0.1	--

Source: Bureau of Justice Statistics, National Crime Victimization Survey, 2003–2012.

-- Less than 0.05 or 0.05%.

! Interpret with caution; estimate based on 10 or fewer cases, or the coefficient of variation is greater than 50%.

Appendix Table 4. Standard errors for Table 2: Victims' perceptions of offender bias in hate crimes, 2004, 2011, and 2012

Offender bias	2004	2011	2012
Ethnicity	3.7%	5.2%	5.1%
Race	4.5	5.9	5.1
Association	3.8	5.7	4.7
Religion	2.6	4.8	4.4
Gender	2.9	4.8	4.3
Sexual orientation	3.7	4.3!	3.2
Disability	2.7	4.5	2.8
Perceived characteristics	3.5	3.8!	2.3!

Source: Bureau of Justice Statistics, National Crime Victimization Survey, 2003–2012.

! Interpret with caution; estimate based on 10 or fewer cases, or the coefficient of variation is greater than 50%.

Appendix Table 5. Standard errors for Table 3: Hate and nonhate crime victimizations, by type of crime, 2004, 2011, and 2012

	2004		2011		2012	
Type of crime	Hate	Nonhate	Hate	Nonhate	Hate	Nonhate
Violent	3.8%	0.6%	3.7%	1.1%	3.2%	0.9%
Serious violentcrime	3.2	0.3	5.0	0.6	4.3	0.5
Simple assault	4.6	0.5	5.7	0.9	4.9	0.7
Property	3.6%	0.6%	3.1%	0.7%	2.8%	0.7%

Source: Bureau of Justice Statistics, National Crime Victimization Survey, 2003–2012.

Appendix Table 6. Standard errors for Table 4: Presence of weapons and injuries sustained in violent hate and nonhate crime victimizations, 2004–2012

	Presence of weapon		Any injury sustained	
Year	Hate	Nonhate	Hate	Nonhate
2004	4.3%	0.9%	4.0%	1.0%
2005	4.2!	1.0	4.3	1.1
2006	4.3	1.0	5.2	1.0
2007	4.2	1.0	4.5	1.1
2008	4.5	1.2	4.2	1.3
2009	5.9	1.7	4.7	1.9
2010	5.5	1.7	3.6	2.0
2011	5.0	1.6	4.7	1.7
2012	4.3	1.3	4.0	1.4

Source: Bureau of Justice Statistics, National Crime Victimization Survey, 2003–2012.

! Interpret with caution; estimate based on 10 or fewer cases, or the coefficient of variation is greater than 50%.

Appendix Table 7. Standard errors for Table 5: Hate crime victimizations reported to police, 2004, 2011, and 2012

		Total			Violent	
	2004	2011	2012	2004	2011	2012
Reported	4.5%	4.8%	4.7%	5.0%	5.1%	4.9%
By victim	3.9	3.9	4.0	3.5	4.1	4.1
Bysomeoneelse	3.6	2.9	3.0	4.4	3.2	3.2
Not reported	4.6%	5.3%	5.1%	5.1%	5.6%	5.3%
Complaint signed	3.0%	3.3%	3.1%	3.7%	3.6%	3.4%
Arrest made	2.5%	2.3%	1.8%!	3.2%	2.4%!	1.9%!

Source: Bureau of Justice Statistics, National Crime Victimization Survey, 2003–2012.

! Interpret with caution; estimate based on 10 or fewer cases, or the coefficient of variation is greater than 50%.

Appendix Table 8. Standard errors for Table 6: Characteristics of violent hate crime victims, 2004, 2011, and 2012

Percent				Rate		
Victim characteristic	2004	2011	2012	2004	2011	2012
Sex						
Male	5.0%	6.1%	5.3%	0.2	0.2	0.2
Female	5.0	6.0	5.3	0.1	0.1	0.2
Race/Hispanic origin						
White	4.5%	6.0%	5.3%	0.1	0.1	0.1
Black/African American	1.8 !	3.7 !	3.3	0.1 !	0.3!	0.3
Hispanic/Latino	3.8	3.5	4.7	0.3	0.2	0.4
Other	2.2 !	3.3 !	2.1 !	0.4 !	0.4!	0.3!
Age						
12–17	4.8%	5.0%	4.3%	0.5	0.5	0.6
18–24	4.0	3.2	4.2	0.4	0.2	0.5
25–34	3.5	5.7	3.1	0.2	0.4	0.2
35–49	4.3	4.3	4.0	0.2	0.2	0.2
50–64	2.8	3.4	4.1	0.1	0.1	0.2
65 or older	1.1 !	1.1 !	0.9 !	0.1 !	0.1!	0.1!
Household income						
$24,999 or less	4.8%	5.8%	4.8%	0.3	0.4	0.4
$25,000–$49,999	4.3	4.0	3.5	0.2	0.2	0.2
$50,000 or more	4.5	4.4	5.1	0.1	0.1	0.2
Not reported	3.8	5.2	3.6	0.2	0.2	0.2

Source: Bureau of Justice Statistics, National Crime Victimization Survey, 2003–2012.

! Interpret with caution; estimate based on 10 or fewer cases, or the coefficient of variation is greater than 50%.

Appendix Table 9. Standard errors for Table 7: Characteristics of violent hate crime offenders as reported by victims, 2004, 2011, and 2012

Offender characteristic	2004	2011	2012
Number of offenders			
One	4.7%	6.1%	5.2%
Two or more	4.5	6.0	4.9
Unknown	1.4 !	0.6 !	1.3 !
Sex			
Male	4.9%	6.0%	5.3%
Female	4.5	4.9	3.6
Both male and female	1.6 !	3.2 !	2.5 !

Offender characteristic	2004	2011	2012
Unknown	1.8 !	1.3 !	3.5 !
Race			
White	4.6%	6.1%	4.9%
Black/African American	5.0	5.0	4.8
Other	3.8	2.2 !	3.7 !
Various races	2.5 !	2.6 !	2.2 !
Unknown	2.3 !	2.4 !	3.1 !
Age			
17 or younger	4.6%	4.8%	3.9%
18–29	4.0	5.3	3.3
30 or older	4.3	5.6	5.2
Two or more age groups	4.2	2.9 !	3.0
Unknown	2.3 !	2.4 !	3.7 !
Relationship to victim			
Intimate/family/casual acquaintance	5.1%	6.1%	5.3%
Stranger	5.0	5.6	5.2
Unknown	3.1 !	2.4 !	2.4 !

Source: Bureau of Justice Statistics, National Crime Victimization Survey, 2003–2012.

! Interpret with caution; estimate based on 10 or fewer cases, or the coefficient of variation is greater than 50%.

Appendix Table 10. Standard errors for Table 8: Hate crime victimizations recorded bythe NCVS and UCR,2004–2012

	NCVS	
Year	Not reported to police	Reported to police
2004	26,809	24,716
2005	25,442	23,689
2006	26,136	24,519
2007	28,894	24,266
2008	32,896	27,174
2009	44,352	34,455
2010	43,032	25,336
2011	35,142	17,239
2012	35,004	24,399

Source: Bureau of Justice Statistics, National Crime Victimization Survey, 2003–2012.

INDEX

#

9/11, 60

A

Abraham, 16
access, 51
acquaintance, 79, 91
ADC, 60
adjustment, 83
Administrative Procedure Act, 46
advocacy, 8
Africa, 13
African Americans, 12, 34, 43
African-American, 23, 42
age, 10, 26, 33, 40, 50, 52, 54, 59, 69, 72, 76, 77, 78, 80, 82, 83, 85, 87, 91
agencies, vii, 2, 3, 4, 8, 25, 26, 29, 30, 35, 56, 85, 86
Alaska, 6, 13, 77, 79
Algeria, 13
Americans with Disabilities Act, 10
anger, 35
Anti-Defamation League, 57, 59, 67
anus, 53
arrest(s), 10, 24, 30, 75
arson, 4, 18, 43, 45, 78, 80, 81
Asia, 14
assault, 22, 23, 24, 45, 47, 53, 54, 69, 72, 73, 74, 77, 79, 80, 81, 82, 87, 89
atheists, 14, 35
attachment, 13, 51
attacker, 24
Attorney General, 3, 45, 46, 86
authority, 3, 16, 45, 48, 49
awareness, 2, 5

B

backlash, 60
Bahrain, 13
Bangladesh, 62
behaviors, 11
benefits, 49
Bhutan, 62
bias, vii, 1, 2, 4, 5, 7, 8, 9, 10, 11, 12, 17, 18, 21, 24, 25, 26, 28, 31, 32, 33, 34, 35, 36, 37, 38, 39, 40, 41, 42, 43, 44, 45, 54, 56, 58, 59, 61, 62, 69, 70, 71, 72, 74, 75, 77, 79, 80, 81, 85, 86, 88
Bible, 15, 16
BJS, 69, 71, 82, 84, 85
Blacks, 12, 34
blame, 63
bones, 47, 48, 53, 75
brain, 10
breakdown, 40
brothers, 23
Bureau of Justice Statistics (BJS), 69, 70, 71, 72, 74, 75, 77, 79, 80, 81, 82, 87, 88, 89, 90, 91
burn, 18, 43, 53
businesses, 78

C

Cambodia, 13
Caribbean, 62
category a, 12, 34, 53
Catholic Church, 15
Catholics, 14, 35
Census, 1, 13, 14, 82, 84
Chicago, 65
China, 13
Christianity, 15, 16
civil rights, 57
classification, 40
classroom, 23
clothing, 11, 21, 41, 58, 62
coefficient of variation, 72, 74, 76, 77, 79, 85, 88, 89, 90, 91
coercion, 50, 54
collaboration, 56
color, 3, 12, 34, 47, 63
coma, 19
commercial, 50, 51, 54
communities, 1, 17, 60, 63
community, 3, 5, 8, 13, 18, 21, 23, 24, 36, 37, 39, 43, 44, 45, 60, 63
community conflict, 63
community relations, 60
community service, 5
compilation, 3
compliance, 56
concussion, 21, 44
conference, 22
Congress, 3, 46, 71, 86
consent, 48, 50, 52, 53, 54
construction, 53
consulting, 63
controlled substances, 48
conviction, 22
cooperation, 3, 86
cosmetic, 10
Costa Rica, 13
covering, 7, 38, 86
crimes, 1, 2, 3, 4, 5, 29, 33, 37, 40, 45, 46, 47, 57, 58, 59, 61, 69, 70, 71, 73, 75, 78, 80, 81, 82, 85, 86
criminal justice system, 82
critical value, 46
cultivation, 48
culture, 12, 13, 34, 61
customers, 51

D

data collection, 1, 2, 3, 5, 26, 54, 82, 85, 86
deaths, 53
decision-making process, 4, 35, 37
demographic characteristics, vii
demonstrations, 39
Department of Justice, 63, 64, 65, 66
destruction, 30, 45, 49, 80, 81
detention, 50
directives, 56
disability, 3, 5, 7, 8, 9, 10, 28, 33, 34, 36, 38, 39, 45, 46, 47, 56, 63, 69, 85
discrimination, 46
disorder, 10
distribution, 48, 85
District of Columbia, 86
diversity, 56
Dominican Republic, 13
draft, 57
drugs, 48

E

East Asia, 62
economic consequences, 82
education, 82
egg, 11
Egypt, 13
electronic communications, 49
e-mail, 56
employees, 20
endocrine, 10
enforcement, 2, 3, 4, 5, 25, 29, 32, 35, 57, 63
environment, 60
equality, 2
equipment, 48, 49, 50, 53

ethnic groups, 61
ethnicity, 1, 3, 5, 7, 8, 9, 10, 12, 14, 23, 26, 28, 33, 34, 36, 38, 39, 42, 45, 56, 59, 60, 61, 69, 71, 85, 86
Europe, 14
evidence, 3, 8, 19, 20, 21, 22, 24, 37, 41, 44, 45, 69, 71, 86
expertise, 32
explosives, 52

F

fairness, 2
faith, 14, 15, 16, 17, 24, 39, 62
family life, 46
fasting, 15
FBI, vii, 1, 2, 3, 4, 5, 9, 12, 17, 18, 26, 28, 31, 32, 34, 35, 39, 56, 57, 59, 69, 78, 80, 81, 85, 86
fear, 35, 48, 51, 53, 54, 60
Federal Bureau of Investigation, 1
federal law, 2
Filipino, 13
financial, 46
firearms, 52
fiscal year, 46
flexibility, 26
force, 49, 50, 51, 53, 54
fraud, 50, 53, 54

G

gambling, 49, 50
gay men, 9, 17, 22
gender identity, 3, 5, 7, 8, 9, 10, 11, 12, 23, 28, 33, 34, 36, 38, 39, 40, 42, 45, 47, 56, 57, 58, 59, 63, 69, 71, 85, 86
gender role, 21
gestures, 7, 38
God, 15, 16
governments, 15
graffiti, 7, 20, 22, 38, 42
grouping, 12, 34
Guam, 13, 66
guardian, 50
guidance, 18, 56, 60
guidelines, vii, 2, 45, 56

H

hair, 11, 12, 17, 21, 24, 34, 43, 63
Hamas, 61
harassment, 23
hate crime, vii, 2, 3, 4, 5, 7, 8, 9, 18, 22, 25, 26, 29, 30, 31, 32, 33, 35, 36, 37, 38, 39, 40, 44, 54, 56, 57, 58, 60, 61, 62, 63, 69, 70, 71, 72, 73, 75, 76, 77, 78, 79, 80, 81, 85, 86, 87, 88, 90
Hawaii, 13
health, 46
heredity, 10, 12, 33, 34
heterosexuality, 46
Hezbollah, 61
high school, 24
Hispanics, 76
history, 22
Hmong, 13
homes, 16
homosexuality, 46
hospitalization, 75
hostility, 10, 22, 34
House, 22, 64
human, 2, 50, 53

I

identity, 12, 25, 36, 46, 49, 57, 62
ideology, 12, 34
image, 43
imitation, 48
in transition, 18, 43
income, 76, 77, 82, 90
India, 13, 15, 44, 62
individuals, 3, 11, 17, 19, 34, 41, 58, 60, 70
injure, 48, 54
injuries, 74, 75, 89
injury, 10, 23, 33, 44, 47, 48, 53, 73, 74, 75, 82, 89

institutions, 78
intimidation, 45, 54, 78, 80, 81
Iraq, 13
iron, 19
Islam, 15
isolation, 35
issues, 60

J

Japan, 13
Jews, 14, 20, 25, 35
Jordan, 13
justification, 16
juveniles, 5, 40, 45, 46, 80, 86

K

kill, 53
Korea, 13
Kuwait, 13

L

laceration, 47, 48, 53
language barrier, 60
law enforcement, vii, 2, 3, 4, 14, 18, 21, 25, 26, 30, 31, 32, 35, 37, 44, 56, 57, 59, 60, 63, 85, 86
laws, 15, 16, 48, 51, 52
lead, 5, 7, 28, 38
learning, 10, 31, 58
learning disabilities, 10
Lebanon, 13
legislation, 5, 71
light, 42, 60
loss of consciousness, 47, 48, 53, 75

M

major decisions, 15
majority, 61, 62, 78
Malaysia, 13
management, 56
manslaughter, 45, 78, 80, 81
marital status, 82
marriage, 52
materials, 15, 32
matter, 53
Mauritania, 13
mediation, 63
medical, 19, 21, 42
medical care, 42
mental illness, 10
mental impairment, 10, 33
merchandise, 51
Miami, 65
Microsoft, 26, 29, 30, 31
Middle East, 14, 61
military, 82
misunderstanding, 61
misuse, 49
model system, 32
modules, 31
modus operandi, 39
Morocco, 13
Moses, 16
motivation, vii, 1, 5, 8, 24, 25, 26, 28, 31, 36, 37, 38, 43, 45, 71
murder, 45, 54, 78, 80, 81
musculoskeletal, 10
Muslims, 15, 24, 62

N

narcotic, 48
narcotics, 48
National Defense Authorization Act, 5, 47
National Incident-Based Reporting System (NIBRS), 25, 26
national origin, 12, 34, 47, 61, 63, 85
NCVS, vii, 69, 70, 78, 80, 81, 82, 83, 84, 85, 91
Nepal, 62
New England, 64
NIBRS, 10, 25, 26, 27, 28, 29, 36, 47, 59
North Africa, 14, 61
nurses, 21

O

offenders, vii, 7, 8, 9, 20, 22, 24, 25, 26, 31, 38, 42, 43, 44, 45, 56, 59, 77, 78, 79, 85, 86, 90
Office of Management and Budget, 12, 34, 56
OMB, 12, 34, 56
operations, 56
organ(s), 10, 53
outreach, 60, 63
oversight, 56
overweight, 4

P

Pacific, 6, 13, 77, 79
Pakistan, 13, 62
parents, 3
participants, 26
perpetrators, 20, 22, 23, 43, 58, 61
personal relations, 14
personal relationship, 14
persons with disabilities, 4, 86
Philadelphia, 64
photographs, 51
physical characteristics, 12, 34
physical health, 36, 39
police, vii, 22, 24, 39, 43, 60, 61, 70, 72, 74, 75, 76, 77, 78, 79, 80, 81, 82, 87, 89, 91
policy, vii, 2, 46
population, 36, 56, 72, 83, 85, 86, 87
prejudice, 3, 45, 69, 86
preparation, 48
President, 47, 56
primacy, 15, 16
principles, 16, 56
professionals, 36, 39
profit, 49
pronunciation, 61
property crimes, 72, 76, 82, 83, 87
proposition, 37
Protestants, 14, 35
publishing, 51
Puerto Rico, 64
purification, 14

R

race, 3, 4, 5, 6, 7, 8, 9, 10, 12, 13, 14, 19, 23, 26, 28, 33, 34, 36, 38, 39, 42, 45, 47, 56, 59, 60, 61, 63, 69, 82, 85, 86
radio, 40
Ramadan, 15
rape, 31, 45, 54, 69, 72, 74, 75, 77, 79, 80, 81, 82, 87
reading, 61
reality, 14
recall, 83
reception, 20
recommendations, 56
reliability, 70, 84, 85
religion, 3, 4, 5, 7, 8, 9, 10, 12, 14, 15, 16, 17, 22, 24, 28, 33, 34, 36, 38, 39, 42, 45, 46, 47, 56, 60, 61, 63, 69, 85, 86
religious beliefs, 14, 35
reputation, 49
requirement(s), 15, 26, 37
residential neighborhood, 21
resolution, 37
resource management, 56
resources, 5, 36, 39, 56
response, 3, 35, 56, 83

S

safety, 60
Samoa, 13
sample design, 83, 84
sampling error, 84
Saudi Arabia, 13
school, 8, 24, 46, 62, 76
security, 46
seizure, 50
sensitivity, 35
services, 36, 50, 63, 64
sex, 11, 17, 18, 41, 50, 51, 53, 54, 58, 59, 82
sexual activities, 51

sexual intercourse, 52
sexual orientation, 3, 4, 5, 7, 8, 9, 10, 17, 23, 25, 28, 33, 34, 35, 36, 38, 39, 40, 42, 45, 46, 47, 56, 57, 58, 63, 69, 85, 86
significance level, 84
signs, 19, 44, 62
skin, 3, 10, 12, 34
slavery, 50, 54
social standing, 49
society, 11, 36, 80, 81, 86
Somalia, 13
South America, 13
South Asia, 17, 60, 62, 63
Southeast Asia, 13
specifications, 29
speech, 9, 10
Sri Lanka, 13, 62
stability, 70
standard error, 70, 72, 74, 76, 77, 79, 80, 81, 84, 85, 87
state(s), 2, 3, 4, 18, 35, 41, 43, 47, 86
statistics, vii, 3, 5, 40, 85
steel, 17
stereotypes, 21, 61
street gang, 19
structure, 48, 53
style, 43
Sudan, 13
suicide, 61
supervisor, 37
syndrome, 10
Syria, 13

T

target, 43
Task Force, 57, 68
teeth, 47, 48, 53, 75
telephone, 40, 64
tensions, 7, 38, 63
test procedure, 84
Thailand, 13
theft, 20, 48, 50, 51, 53, 70, 72, 74, 80, 81, 82, 83, 87
threats, 24, 40, 42
trade, 51
traditions, 15
trafficking, 50
training, 1, 2, 32, 57, 60, 63, 64
training programs, 32, 64
transport, 49, 50, 51
transportation, 48, 50, 52, 54

U

uniform, 3
universe, 14, 35
updating, 31

V

vagina, 53
vandalism, 39, 45, 61, 78, 80, 81
victimization, vii, 69, 70, 71, 72, 76, 82, 83, 84, 85, 87
victims, vii, 5, 7, 18, 19, 21, 22, 23, 26, 31, 37, 38, 57, 59, 60, 61, 69, 70, 71, 72, 74, 75, 76, 77, 78, 79, 80, 81, 85, 90
Vietnam, 13
violence, 51, 53, 61, 73, 83
violent crime, 69, 72, 73, 74, 75, 87

W

walking, 9, 20, 21, 41, 43
Washington, 64, 66, 67, 68
weapons, 52, 74, 82, 89
web, 82, 84
welfare, 49
well-being, 46
witnesses, 21, 22, 37, 60, 61

Y

Yemen, 13